KICK IT!

Stop Smoking In 5 Days

Judy Perlmutter
Founder of
Habit Breakers Program

Published by HPBooks
A Division of HPBooks, Inc.
P.O. Box 5367, Tucson, AZ 85703
602/888-2150
ISBN: 0-89586-456-8
Library of Congress Catalog No. 85-73828
©1986 Judy Perlmutter   Printed in U.S.A.
1st Printing

W9-CDI-307

To Joe, Michael and Matthew: With all my love.

I want to thank the following for their support:
Jack Artenstein
Jim Friedberg, Esq.
Dr. Jack Goldin
Angela Hynes
Shelley Levinson
Ira Ritter
Albie Rosenhaus
Sharon Rosenhaus

Special thanks to my parents Leslie and Susan Rosenberg, my mother-in-law Olga Perlmutter and my grandparents Edith and Imre Krausz.

Publisher
Rick Bailey

Executive Editor
Theodore DiSante

Editor
Carol Worth

Art Director
Don Burton

Cover Design
Kathleen Koopman

Production Coordinator
Cindy Coatsworth

Typography
Michelle Carter

Director of Manufacturing
Anthony B. Narducci

NOTICE: The information contained in this book is true and complete to the best of our knowledge. The author and publisher disclaim all liability in connection with the use of this information.

CONTENTS

Foreword

As a child, I was always pestering my parents to quit smoking—more out of concern for my own well-being than compassion for their health. I remember sitting in the back seat of my parent's Chevy, dodging burning ashes from my father's lit cigarette dangling out the window. Once, I was burned so badly by an ash that I developed a huge blister. It was a tough choice between being burned with the window open or suffocating from smoke with the window closed.

In spite of my dread of cigarettes, I smoked my first when I was 12. I asked my father when I could start smoking. He looked squarely into my eyes, and said, "Right now, sweetheart. Let's smoke together." I knew he had something up his sleeve when he lit my first one for me. I smoked two cigarettes—it felt like half a pack—and turned green. I was close to throwing up when he asked me if I'd like another. Needless to say, that was the beginning and the end of my smoking experience.

A pack-and-a-half-a-day smoker for over 35 years, my 55-year-old father smoked through two strokes, carotid artery surgery, and a coronary triple bypass. He finally quit after the bypass, but not because he was afraid of dying. For some reason, cigarettes didn't taste good after his last surgery. I'll never forget watching him try to readdict himself just two days out of intensive care. He actually would hold the pillow to his chest as he tried to ease the pain of coughing.

My 52-year-old mother also had problems aggravated by her smoking habit. Smoking a pack a day for 25 years didn't help her damaged heart—she had rheumatic fever as a child. She, too, underwent open-heart surgery, and later required a pacemaker to regulate her heartbeat. She finally quit the habit because she got angry at being controlled by cigarettes.

If there's one thing I learned from years of pleading with my parents to quit smoking, it's this: You can't talk someone out of the smoking habit. Pleading, bribery, threats, and scare tactics don't work. Perhaps they haven't worked on you either.

Prior to starting Habit Breakers in 1979, I investigated and worked for smoking-cessation clinics. I was surprised at what I found: Smokers quitting the habit? Yes. Staying off cigarettes? No. Program participants were relapsing faster than the counselors could treat them—more than half of smoking-cessation program participants are smoking again within six months! According to *Addic-*

tions: Issues and Answers, after one year, 65% to 75% of the participants at most clinics return to smoking.

The reasons? They aren't taught effective ways of dealing with the urge to smoke. They aren't adequately shown how to prevent relapse. And they aren't given or taught to set up a solid support system to help them stay non-smokers. It seemed that most programs were more interested in short-term, not long-term, success.

The Habit Breakers Stop Smoking Program is different. It's a proven, step-by-step method with a success rate of 80% in the first year. And this success rate has held for the five years Habit Breakers has been in business! I base my program on my research and experience in smoking-cessation, in addition to my education in psychology from UCLA.

In this book I share my trade secrets. Here's why: First, this is too good a program to keep to myself and my clients. Second, I realize that many of you don't want to go to a clinic for help, and prefer to quit alone at home. And finally, if this book can save your life, or improve the quality of your life it will have been worth writing.

Wishing you the best of health,

Judy Perlmutter

Judy Perlmutter
Founder of Habit Breakers

Introduction: What To Expect From This Book

By the time you finish this chapter, you will be prepared to stop smoking. By the time you finish the second chapter, you will be an ex-smoker. And, by the time you complete this five day plan, you will know how to stay off cigarettes—Permanently!

This is more than just a how-to-quit-smoking book. It's your breakthrough to kicking the habit once and for all and losing the desire to resume. This step-by-step, gut-level approach to quitting consists of a series of exercises that take the charm and the power out of your smoking habit. This book shows you how to "turn off" to smoking, as you "turn on" to relaxing.

IT WORKS FOR EVERYONE

This program works whether you smoke five cigarettes a day, or five packs a day; whether you've been smoking for one year or 65 years; whether you smoke cigarettes, pipes, or cigars. In the course of the program I refer to cigarettes exclusively, but I also mean any type of nicotine-based tobacco smoked.

The program works if you're quitting for the first time, or if you've quit and relapsed many times before. It works regardless of how much you smoke, how long you've been smoking, and how many times you've tried to quit. It works because it deals effectively with all the problems that confront you, the quitter:

1) The chemical and psychological addiction to cigarettes.
2) The nagging urge to smoke.
3) Learning to relax without smoking
4) Weight control.
5) Backsliding into smoking.
6) On-going support.

The Habit Breakers "Kick It" 5-Day Stop-Smoking Plan is an active approach to breaking the smoking habit. By participating in a series of exercises that turn you off to smoking, you will break the chain of positive associations you've built up over time. You will be free from the power of this addiction once and for all!

WHY QUIT SMOKING?

Perhaps I don't have to tell you that cultural attitudes toward smoking have changed since you first started. For almost 30 years it was considered fashionable, sophisticated, and even sexy to smoke.

Then, in the late 60's and early 70's, Americans began to take a different view of smoking. We learned that 1 out of 10 heavy smokers will develop lung cancer. We learned that 30% of all cancer deaths are directly related to smoking. We learned that smoking doubles the risk of heart attack and greatly increases risks of stillbirths and miscarriages. We learned that smoking results in 340,000 premature deaths every year.

Now in the 80's, smoking is not fashionable. The habit that was once cinematically considered cool and confident is now used to convey nervousness, weakness, or even malevolence.

Anti-smoking laws are beginning to spring up across the country. Non-smoking patrons in restaurants are demanding to be seated apart from smokers. Non-smoking airline passengers are complaining of the "sidestream" smoke drifting over from the smoking section. Businesses are helping employees to stop smoking. Corporations have done studies and found that the average smoking employee costs the company an extra $4,600 per year in increased medical costs and absenteeism.

More and more smokers are deciding that their habit is neither fashionable, sophisticated, sexy, nor convenient. On the contrary. Today, smoking means social discrimination, bad breath, stained teeth, wrinkled skin, burned clothes, nagging from family, friends, and physician, hard-earned money gone up in smoke, lethargy, smoker's cough, and disease and death for many. This package deal is a lot more than smokers bargained for. As a matter of fact, it's a lot more than *you* bargained for, and you want out of this habit once and for all! That's why you bought this book, and that's why you're going to quit smoking.

HOW THE PROGRAM WORKS

Today you are going to select your *"Kick It" Week* and put aside five consecutive days to devote about 30 minutes each day to this program.

You will stop smoking right after you finish Day 1 of "Kick It" Week, although *you will be smoking* during your scheduled half-hour sessions for the first three days of the program. But that means no smoking between appointments. The smoking you will do is designed to "turn off" your desire to smoke.

When you end Day 1, you will put your cigarette out for 24 hours until Day 2, when you will be instructed to smoke again, "turn off" style.

You will smoke your last cigarette during your scheduled time on Day 3. But until your "Kick It" Week starts, feel free to smoke as much as you like.

Each day of "Kick It" Week you will be signing a 24-hour "contract" to help you quit smoking. And from time to time, you will be doing some written exercises. To get the results you want, you must fully participate in each day's exercise.

For the first three days of the program you will

need to have some supplies with you for the session. At the end of each day's session I tell you what supplies are needed for the following day.

All major instructions are in bold lettering like that below. This way you won't miss anything. And certain exercises must be read thoroughly first before participating in them.

TAKE 15 MINUTES TO PREPARE YOURSELF FOR QUITTING SMOKING BY READING THE NEXT CHAPTER NOW.

Setting Your "Kick It" Dates

You've thought about it. You've talked about it. Perhaps you've made several attempts at it. If you're serious about quitting smoking, there's only one thing left to do—and that's DO IT!

Unless you've just recently lost a loved one, or you're in the midst of a divorce or other stress that may interfere with your success, the best time to quit smoking is NOW! It's a fact of human nature that the longer you put off your decision to quit, the less likely you ever will. Let's not waste any time.

GET YOUR CALENDAR, AND JOIN ME BACK HERE AS SOON AS YOU HAVE IT IN FRONT OF YOU.

The first thing you need to do is choose five consecutive days that you can devote to the *"Kick It" 5-Day, Stop-Smoking Plan*. If you work Monday through Friday from 9:00 a.m. to 5:00 p.m., **I** suggest you schedule your first session for a Saturday morning. This way you can have the luxury of the weekend to recuperate from the symptoms of nicotine withdrawal. In addition, you can take time to relax and pamper yourself.

To help adjust to the chemical changes your body will undergo, I also suggest that you schedule your 30-minute sessions at the same time each day. That is, if you begin your program on Saturday at 9:00 a.m., your next session should be planned for Sunday at 9:00 a.m., and the third for Monday at 9:00 a.m., and so on.

While you have your calendar in front of you, check your "Kick It" Week again. See if you can cancel or postpone any stressful meetings or social events in which people will be smoking and drinking. To be completely safe, stay away from smokers for the first three days of the program. If you live with smokers, stay away from them when they're smoking, or ask them not to smoke around you. And stay away from alcohol too because it weakens your resolve. Without temptation, it's easier to keep your commitment to stop smoking.

PAMPERING YOURSELF
DURING "KICK IT" WEEK

Who says your "Kick It" Week has to be horrible? You can either feel out of control, angry, deprived and obsessed with the thought of a cigarette, spending your time counting the urges to smoke, or. . .

You can surprise yourself and turn "Kick It" Week into a challenging opportunity to create new, more fulfilling ways to relax and reward yourself.

Imagine getting up bright and early on the morning of the first day of "Kick It" Week, starting out with a wholesome and delicious breakfast, completing your first stop-smoking session, taking a fresh brisk walk or jog in the park to get your energy and enthusiasm going, spending a relaxing day doing your favorite activities, dining by candlelight, and settling into a nice hot tub before you go to sleep. Imagine five days filled with massages, facials, manicures, creams, hot baths, jacuzzis and saunas. Make this week special. Make an appointment to get a new haircut, or go shopping for some new clothes to suit your new non-smoking image.

Treat yourself to some extra sleep. Treat your body to some stretching, yoga, or dancing. Get the circulation going with vigorous exercise like jogging, swimming, or aerobics classes. Now's a good time to join a health club and start on a regular exercise program.

Go all out for yourself! Buy yourself a bouquet of flowers. This may be the first time in a long time you'll be able to smell their full aroma. Spend a wonderfully relaxing evening at home. Dine by candlelight. See a movie. Visit friends. Relax and listen to your favorite music. Take up an old hobby or start a new one. Ever think of getting involved in photography, drawing, painting, ceramics, gardening, cooking, sewing, mechanics, carpentry, computers, writing, or reading?

As you go through the process of quitting smoking, it's within your power to portray yourself as either a suffering, frustrated addict in the throes of withdrawal, or as an optimistic, clean, and proud person venturing out in a brave, new, non-smoking world. The way you treat yourself this week will be expressed in how you look, act, and feel. And the way others respond to you depends on your attitude about quitting. It can either be something you force yourself to do, or something that your're lucky enough to be able to do.

Quitting smoking can illicit comments like: "You look like hell. You look like you're quitting smoking." Or it can illicit comments like: "What happened to you? You look great! I thought you were quitting smoking this week!"

Quitting smoking can draw comments like: "I better keep away from you. You're dangerous this week." Or it can draw comments like: "You're acting so wonderful. I can't believe you've just quit smoking!"

Be good to yourself during "Kick It" Week, and it will pay off in how you feel about yourself, and how others feel about you.

WARNING: STAY WITH YOUR "KICK IT" WEEK

It's vitally important to not change your "Kick It" Week dates. The success of this program is built on your willingness to *keep your word to yourself.*

Doing so reflects the level of importance you give this challenge. It's most important that you build your success on a solid foundation, so give quitting smoking the priority it deserves—that you deserve—and reap the benefits of your success.

Choose your dates and stick to them without exception. Follow through step by step and free yourself from your smoking habit. You'll make it through because it's completely within your power to do so!

ON THE NEXT PAGE IS A STOP-SMOKING CONTRACT. FILL IT OUT AFTER YOU'VE CHOSEN YOUR "KICK IT" DATES.

STOP-SMOKING CONTRACT

I, _____ hereby commit to stop smoking by completing the *Habit Breakers "Kick It" 5-Day, Stop-Smoking Plan*. I promise to follow all the instructions assigned, and devote 30 minutes a day for five consecutive days to the program.

My "Kick It" Week is scheduled for Day 1 _____, Day 2 _____, Day 3 _____, Day 4 _____, Day 5 _____. I will not change these dates.

I understand that if I fail to adhere to all the instructions in the program, then I assume total responsibility for readdicting myself.

Signed _____

Date _____

BUILDING MOTIVATION

You may be surprised to learn that most smokers who decide to quit the habit don't do so because they're afraid of dying from a smoking-related disease. Fear of cancer, heart attack, emphysema, stroke, or the many other smoking-related diseases is perceived by most smokers as something that only happens to the other smoker. Unless it's already happened to you, or there's reason to believe that there's immediate danger, the link between smoking and disease rarely hits home.

Most smokers quit for more personal reasons. Some time ago, an 80-year-old man came to see me about quitting smoking. He had been smoking a pack a day since he was 13 years old, and had a history of stroke, high blood pressure, and bad circulation.

On the questionnaire beside "How important is it for you to stop smoking?" he answered "It's urgent that I quit immediately." So I asked him why, after 67 years of smoking and living through a stroke did he feel such urgency to quit now? Interestingly, he replied that it wasn't because he was afraid of another stroke. If it was his fate, he would accept that. And it wasn't because he was afraid of dying.

In fact, he told me outright that the idea of dropping dead tomorrow wouldn't bother him at all. He wanted to quit because he couldn't sleep due to his smoker's cough, and he just couldn't bear another night of interrupted sleep. In his case, the coughing, pain and the inconvenience of getting up in the middle of the night motivated him to quit.

Before you put your cigarettes out for good, it's important to know *why* you're quitting smoking. Starting today, you're going to use these reasons to build motivation and reinforce your decision to quit. Once, I had to remind a client three times in the course of five minutes why she had decided to quit. It's so easy to forget the importance of quitting when there's that temptation to have "just one puff" on a cigarette. That's why I've designed the following exercise to help you reinforce your reasons for quitting.

Let's look at why you've chosen to give up smoking. Simply put, there are two basic reasons why you're quitting smoking:

1) The consequences of smoking.
2) The benefits of quitting.

On the one hand, you're quitting because you're no longer willing to put up with certain consequences of smoking. Perhaps you've had it with the coughing, the lack of energy, or the smell of your body, hair, clothing and breath. Perhaps you're beginning to feel like a social outcast in a world that's becoming less and less tolerant of smokers. Whatever it is that's personally turning you off to your habit, one thing's certain—you've come to a point where the consequences are beginning to, or already have, outweighed the need to continue smoking.

On the other hand, you're quitting because there are certain benefits, or payoffs, you expect to attain once you've quit. The payoff can be anything from a better game of tennis, or a fresher, younger look, to feeling proud of breaking a serious and destructive habit.

GO THROUGH THE FOLLOWING LISTS OF SMOKING'S CONSEQUENCES AND QUITTING'S BENEFITS. CHECK OFF THE ITEMS THAT APPLY TO YOU.

EMOTIONAL CONSEQUENCES OF SMOKING

____ I feel stressed when I smoke.

____ Smoking depresses me.

____ I don't like using a cigarette to vent my frustrations.

____ I feel emotionally weak because I smoke.

____ I hate giving up my power to a drug.

____ I feel nervous and anxious after smoking.

____ I hate sneaking around trying to hide my smoking.

HEALTH CONSEQUENCES OF SMOKING

Check off the following diseases or conditions that have been caused or aggravated by smoking.

____ Allergies

____ Asthma

____ Dental problems

____ Diabetes

____ Emphysema

____ Heart attack

____ Heart disease

____ High blood pressure

____ Hyperglycemia

____ Pregnancy problems

____ Stroke

____ Ulcer

____ Cough

____ Sinusitus

____ Hoarse or husky voice

____ Irritated eyes

____ Upset stomach

____ Nervousness

____ Dizziness

____ Excess sweating

____ Heart palpitation

____ Chest pains

____ Shortness of breath while resting

____ Swelling of limbs

____ Bad circulation—cold hands and feet

____ Low energy
____ Acid stomach and indigestion
____ Dulled taste and smell
____ Trouble with sexual functioning
____ Trouble breathing deeply
____ Trouble sleeping
____ Constant mucous formation in the chest

SOCIAL CONSEQUENCES OF SMOKING

____ I'm fed up with being the only one among my friends still smoking.

____ I hate feeling like a social outcast.

____ I'm self conscious about my smoker's breath and body odor.

____ I've had it with the nagging from friends, family and doctor to quit.

____ I'm afraid of burning people with cigarettes.

____ I'm not happy working away from non-smoking co-workers.

____ I hate getting in trouble with the boss because of all the smoking breaks I'm taking.

____ My sex life is limited to smokers. Non-smokers don't want to be intimate with me.

_____ I hate worrying about dirtying up other people's homes with my smelly cigarettes.

_____ I feel especially guilty smoking around children.

_____ I hate the image I project as a smoker.

_____ I hate setting a bad example for my children.

☞

IMAGE CONSEQUENCES OF SMOKING

_____ I'm embarrassed by the yellow stains on my teeth and between my fingers.

_____ My skin looks pale and lifeless.

_____ My hair is always limp and smells of smoke.

_____ My hair color is beginning to turn yellow from tar.

_____ The crow's feet wrinkles around my eyes are becoming prominent from years of smoking.

_____ The wrinkles between my eyebrows are growing deeper.

_____ Lines around my lips are developing from all that sucking on a cigarette.

_____ My lips are always chapped and dry.

_____ My eyes are red and irritated, not shiny and glowing like they used to be.

_____ My nose is always dripping.

_____ I look harsh and mean when I smoke.

_____ The whole look that I once thought to be
classy and sophisticated looks classless,
outdated, unsophisticated, and dirty.

[👓]

FINANCIAL CONSEQUENCES OF SMOKING

_____ Cigarettes and other smoking paraphernalia
are costing me a small fortune and I know
I'll continue to pay as much as necessary.

_____ My health insurance premiums are more
expensive than a non-smoker's.

_____ I spend a small fortune on dry-cleaning bills
because my clothes stink from smoke.

_____ I spend a lot of money on carpet, drape and
upholstery cleaning

_____ I'm fed up with all the holes I've burned in
clothing, drapes, and furniture.

_____ I'm spending extra money on shampoo,
cologne, mouthwash, breath mints, and
smoker's toothpaste to take care of the
smoke odor.

_____ I lost a job because they wouldn't hire
smoking employees.

NOTE: If you smoke a pack a day, it costs you
about $450 a year to smoke. And if you smoke two

packs a day, that's $900 a year gone up in smoke.

If you add on the hidden costs of smoking like higher insurance rates, replacing or repairing burned clothing, breath fresheners, and increased medical and dental costs, you'll get a more accurate estimate of the total cost of smoking . . . and the price is going up.

EMOTIONAL BENEFITS OF QUITTING

_____ I will feel calmer without smoking.

_____ I won't feel depressed.

_____ I'll find other more constructive ways of venting my frustrations.

_____ I will feel powerful against this drug. I will have beaten this habit for good.

_____ I'll feel emotionally stronger without my crutch.

_____ If I can quit smoking, I can do anything I set my mind to do.

_____ I won't feel guilty because I'm not sneaking around behind others' backs to smoke.

_____ It will feel good to treat my mind and body with respect.

_____ I will get more done in less time. I won't waste any time stalling or procrastinating with cigarettes.

_____ I will be proud to finally accomplish what I've been promising myself to do for a long time now.

⊂▱⊐

HEALTH BENEFITS OF QUITTING

_____ I will live free of the fear of contracting a smoking-related disease.

_____ My body will have a chance to clean out and recuperate from the destruction of smoking.

_____ I will have a healthier pregnancy, and my baby won't suffer the consequences of my smoking habit.

_____ My smoker's cough will disappear.

_____ My nasal drip will cease.

_____ My smoking-related dental problems will disappear.

_____ My stomach will feel better.

_____ Smoking will no longer deplete my body of essential vitamins.

_____ My energy level will be higher.

_____ I will sleep better.

_____ My chest will feel less congested—no more mucous build-up.

27

____ My throat won't feel dry and scratchy.

____ I won't have problems with indigestion.

____ My hoarse voice will clear up.

____ My dental health will be much improved.

____ I won't feel dizzy in the morning because of lighting up.

____ I won't have to worry about shortness of breath while resting.

____ Heart palpitations will go away.

____ I won't sweat as much.

____ Swelling of the limbs will disappear.

____ My circulation will improve and my hands and feet will be warmer.

____ I'll be able to breathe deeper and get more oxygen into my system.

____ My sexual functioning will improve.

____ My sense of taste and smell will improve.

____ I'll be calmer without all that nicotine stimulating my system.

____ I'll add about eight years to my lifespan.

SOCIAL BENEFITS OF QUITTING

____ I'll join the ranks of the non-smokers.

____ I won't feel like a social outcast.

____ I'll be more open to hugs and kisses—giving and receiving—I won't worry about the way I smell.

____ My family, friends and doctor will be proud of me.

____ I won't worry about burning others, or myself with cigarettes.

____ I won't be separated at work, in restaurants, or on airplanes from my non-smoking friends.

____ I'll be more productive at work.

____ My social life will open up to non-smokers.

____ I won't worry about dirtying up other people's homes with my smoke.

____ I won't make excuses for not going to a non-smoker's social engagement.

____ I will see the endings of movies and plays because I won't excuse myself and smoke, or worse, sit through them and bear the discomfort of needing a cigarette.

____ I will be setting a good example for my children.

IMAGE BENEFITS OF QUITTING

____ When I get my teeth cleaned they will stay white.

____ My fingers will be clean of yellow stains.

____ My tongue won't be coated with tar.

____ My skin will look fresher, pinker, more glowing.

____ My eyes will be clearer and brighter—no more bloodshot eyes.

____ I may even look years younger.

____ My hair will smell cleaner and won't be limp from smoke.

____ I won't have nasal drip.

____ My clothes will look and smell fresher.

____ People will notice when I'm wearing perfume or cologne.

____ My makeup, especially lipstick, will stay on longer.

____ The lines around my eyes and mouth will soften, and I'll certainly be preventing myself from premature aging.

____ I'll have no more bulges in my pockets from carrying around cigarettes.

____ My face will look friendlier, and more open without that cigarette dangling out of my mouth.

____ I will convey more strength, energy, success and confidence as an ex-smoker.

FINANCIAL BENEFITS
OF QUITTING

____ I will save hundreds of dollars a year when I quit smoking.

____ My health insurance premiums will go down.

____ I'll be saving on mouthwash, smoker's toothpaste, lighters, matches, dry cleaning bills, and repaired burns in clothing.

____ I will be a more marketable person— companies are more likely to hire someone who's not costing them an additional $4,600 a year.

☞💲

Now that you know all of the reasons why you're quitting smoking, here's how you're going to use this information to motivate yourself to get results:

GO BACK THROUGH YOUR CHECKLIST AND CIRCLE THE FIVE MOST IMPORTANT CONSEQUENCES YOU'RE NO LONGER WILLING TO PUT UP WITH AS A SMOKER.

ALSO CIRCLE THE FIVE MOST IMPORTANT BENEFITS YOU EXPECT TO ATTAIN ONCE YOU'VE QUIT.

WRITE THEM DOWN ON 3x5 CARDS AND PUT THEM IN AS MANY ROOMS AND PLACES AS YOU LOOK.

PIN THEM UP ALL OVER YOUR HOUSE. PUT ONE IN YOUR PURSE OR WALLET. STICK ONE UP ON YOUR REFRIGERATOR, ON THE BATHROOM MIRROR, OR NEAR YOUR BED. PUT SOME AT YOUR PLACE OF WORK.

DO THIS NOW WHILE YOU'RE GEARED UP FOR ACTION.

REMEMBER: IF YOU WANT TO SEE RESULTS, YOU HAVE TO BE AN ACTIVE PARTICIPANT IN YOUR SUCCESS.

Between now and the start of "Kick It" Week, I'd like you to read through this list each and every opportunity you have. Visualize the consequences you've incurred as a smoker, and the benefits you will attain when you kick the habit. The more you picture what you will love about being an ex-smoker, and the more time you spend dwelling on what you hate about the habit, the more geared up you will be for the big day.

DEVELOPING AN
ATTITUDE FOR SUCCESS

Inside each and every smoker, and you are no exception, is a part of you that I call the addict. The addict is that part of you that wants to close this book and forget about quitting smoking. The addict says, "I'll do it later." It's the part that believes that without cigarettes, you'll get fat; or not be able to cope with your job, your family, or the stress of life. You know the part of you I'm talking about—the compulsive part that believes you need cigarettes, no matter what the consequences to you or your health.

Since the moment you decided to take action against your smoking habit, your addict has been devising a mountain of excuses why you can't quit. The addict needs such defense mechanisms to protect you from the horrible consequences you believe will result from quitting.

Life without cigarettes isn't laden with horrendous consequences, but your addict doesn't know that yet, and isn't going to rest a second until you drop the idea of quitting. And trust me when I tell you that your addict is going to try anything to sabotage your attempt to quit smoking.

Fortunately, you can learn to use your addict to work *for* you instead of *against* you. In the following exercise you will learn how your addict thinks and behaves when it tries to get you to give up the idea of quitting. By learning how to talk to your addict, you can beat it at it's own game.

ADDICT THOUGHTS AND BEHAVIOR

This is what your addict tells you, and this is how you can talk back to it:

Addict—If I quit smoking, I'll get fat. I'd rather be a thin smoker than a fat non-smoker.

Self-Talk—Who am I kidding? There are plenty of smokers who quit the habit and don't gain weight, just as there are plenty of overweight smokers. Smoking is not the answer to weight control. If I put on some excess pounds, I'll do something about it directly instead of using it as an excuse to go back to smoking.

Addict—I've been smoking for too many years. I've tried to quit many times, and I can't even make it through the first two hours without a cigarette. I'm hopeless. Why bother trying?

Self-Talk—Why bother? Because I really don't believe I'm hopeless. I wouldn't have bought this book if I did. More than 30 million Americans have kicked this habit, and some of them were heavier smokers than I. This time I'm going to be brave and endure the temporary discomfort of withdrawal because breaking free from this habit is worth it.

Addict—I can't relax without a cigarette. It's the only reward I give myself during the day. It's the only vice I have.

Self-Talk—If this is the best reward I give myself, then I haven't been very kind to me. What kind of a reward is a cancer stick? It's high time I started treating myself better.

Addict—I'm very shy, and I know that cigarettes make me feel more comfortable socially. I'm afraid I'll act awkward if I don't have my security blanket beside me.

Self-Talk—I recognize the need to become more accepting of myself. It's OK to be shy, and it's OK to be imperfect. This can be a great opportunity to stop hiding behind a cigarette and make new friends.

Addict—I won't be able to work and think without my cigarettes.

Self-Talk—I won't use cigarettes any longer to procrastinate getting down to work or figuring out a problem. I'll be able to work and think better as an ex-smoker. My hands will be free. My mind won't be fogged up with drugs. And I'll have more time to get the job done now that I won't be busy with the smoking ritual. I'm willing to find better ways of relieving stress. Smoking isn't the only way to relax.

Addict—Smoking keeps me from being nasty. If it weren't for smoking, I'd lose control and say the wrong thing, or worse, hurt someone.

Self-Talk—For years I've been shoving down unpleasant feelings with cigarettes. This tension festering inside me has to come out somehow, but it

35

doesn't have to come out in destructive ways. There are other ways to relieve tension.

Addict—Smoking's not so bad for you. My grandfather smoked two packs a day for 70 years and he's still going strong at age 90.

Self-Talk—My grandfather's lucky. Who knows if I'll be lucky too. Smoking is a deadly habit, and I'm not willing to take any chances with my life and health.

TAKE A FEW MINUTES NOW TO EXAMINE YOUR OWN ADDICT TALK. USE THE FOLLOWING SPACE TO BECOME AWARE OF HOW YOUR ADDICT MIND CAN SABOTAGE YOUR SUCCESS.

THEN THINK OF WHAT YOU CAN SAY TO YOURSELF TO EFFECTIVELY COUNTERACT THE SABOTAGE.

Addict_____

_____

Self-Talk_____

_____

Addict_____

_____

Self-Talk_____

_____

Addict_____

_____

Self-Talk_____

_____

Just before the start of "Kick It" Week, you'll find yourself wanting to cancel. Suddenly you'll remember that you have an important business deal to complete. Or you'll remember that your uncle is due in town and you'd rather not put up with his company *and* quitting smoking at the same time. Or you'll run yourself down and get sick with a cold or flu—you'd be amazed at how mind and body work together to sabotage quitting.

I'm not suggesting that there aren't valid reasons for postponing "Kick It" Week. Certainly you'd want to put it off under unbearably stressful circumstances. But what I *am* saying is that life is always full of ups and downs, and there are always going to be reasons quitting now is "out of the question."

If you hear yourself give excuses like "Not now, I have to repair that leak in the roof," or "Not today, I have to shampoo the dog," or "Not now, my horoscope advises against me quitting smoking," you can bet that your addict is working on you.

It's your decision whether or not you give in to your excuses. All I can say again is, the longer you put off acting on your decision to quit smoking, the less likely you are to do so.

LOOK FOR ANY EXCUSES YOU COULD USE TO GET YOURSELF OFF THE HOOK OF QUITTING. LOOK LONG HARD AND DEEP WITHIN YOURSELF.

WRITE DOWN THE APPROPRIATE SELF-TALK TO COMBAT YOUR ADDICT THINKING. REMEMBER: YOU'RE DOING THIS BECAUSE DEEP DOWN INSIDE, YOU TRULY WANT TO KICK THIS HABIT ONCE AND FOR ALL.

Excuse_____

_____

Self-Talk_____

_____

Excuse_____

_____

Self-Talk_____

_____

Excuse_____

_____

Self-Talk_____

_____

SHOPPING THE DAY
BEFORE "KICK IT" WEEK

Before you quit smoking tomorrow, I'd like you to pick up a few items to make "Kick It" Week easier. To make it healthier, buy foods that are low in calories, and high in fiber and nutrition. You want the most bulk and the greatest concentration of nutrients from the fewest calories possible.

In addition, drinking plenty of fluids is important. It helps you eliminate nicotine and other toxins left over from smoking. The more you "flood" your body with fluids, the more toxins you flush out. Urination is an effective way of ridding your body of these chemicals. I recommend the following beverages for "Kick It" Week. Select the items that appeal to you.

Juices—Apple, grapefruit, papaya, mango, boysenberry, peach or apricot nectar, strawberry, cherry, pineapple, and cranberry juice are great. Fresh is always best. If you're concerned about calories, dilute the juice to taste. Also, put it in a lovely wine glass with a sprig of mint or a slice of kiwi to make it feel like a special treat.

Water—Plain, mineral and carbonated are best. Stick with the low-sodium brands to eliminate water retention. Add a twist of lemon or lime for flavor and aroma.

Milk—Whole or skim milk, buttermilk, kefir, or yogurt drinks are recommended. If you're concerned about calories, stay with low-fat products. A nice warm glass of milk in the evening will help calm nerves. Try it with a sprinkle of cinnamon or nutmeg.

Herb Tea—Try anise, boneset, comfrey, elecampane, ginseng, golden seal, pennyroyal or slippery elm. These herbs are especially helpful in soothing lung-associated disorders. Anise, comfrey, and valerian are good for producing a calming effect on the body. Hot or cold, they make for a relaxing break. And if you can't find these ingredients, don't worry. Just about any herb tea will be beneficial.

Vegetables—Eat variety, such as broccoli, cauliflower, beans, carrots, onions, green beans, lettuce— the greener or redder the better— brussel sprouts, spinach, mushrooms, cabbage, celery, zucchini, turnips, beets, radishes, and peppers.

There are lots of interesting vegetables at the supermarket that you may never have tried. This is a good time to experiment and indulge your renewed sense of taste and smell. The easiest and best way to bring out vegetables' natural flavor and beautiful color is to steam them.

Fruits—Have fun with apples, pears, peaches, oranges, tangerines, grapefruits, cherries, pineapples, strawberries, blueberries, boysenberries, nectarines, plums, mangos, papayas, grapes, raspberries, and kiwis. Serve them whole, sliced, or purée them in the blender to make juice. Try them dried too!

Grains—Whole-grain breads, muffins, cereals, barley, and brown rice will be best. They contain more fiber than highly refined foods.

High Protein Foods—Fish, chicken, soybean, eggs, nuts, dairy products, and beans are recommended. Avoid red meat this week because it may make your body *retain* nicotine! This can be a great opportunity for you to start eating a healthier selection of foods if you don't already. What you eat affects not only the way you look, but the way you feel, too.

Low Calorie Snacks—Fruits and vegetables cut up into strips or bite-size pieces, popcorn, rice cakes, crackers, sunflower seeds, gum, and sugarless mints will do. Snacking can help fill the oral need that smoking used to satisfy. Stay with these low-calorie choices, but watch the quantity consumed. Anything eaten in excess can cause you to gain weight and foster compulsive behavior.

EATING RIGHT

While your body is detoxifying through quitting, pay attention to your diet. This is a good time to eat right and give yourself the freshest and healthiest selection of foods possible.

It's a great time to become a label reader too. You'd be amazed at the preservatives and artificial chemicals you consume daily. Also, check the contents for salt and sugar. Minimize your sugar intake to avoid empty calories. Watch the salt consumption so you don't retain water.

If you stick with fresh fruits and vegetables, whole-grain products, chicken and fish (instead of red meats), and low-fat, low-sodium dairy products, you're sure to get the nutrients and fibers you need to keep your energy level high.

Non-food Oral Substitutes—Cinnamon sticks, cloves, straws, toothpicks, and coffee stirrers will do the trick. You don't want to get used to using food to replace your smoking habit, even if it's low-calorie. The things mentioned will help satisfy your oral need.

Tactile Substitutes—If you are more tactile than oral—that is, if you like to fidget with your hands and miss holding something—try a tangible substitute. Hold onto a pen. Doodle with a pencil. Or play with playdough, clay, worry beads, a pocket calculator, or small hand puzzles to fill the void of not smoking.

Vitamins— For the first 30 days of quitting, you should supplement your diet with a good multi-vitamin and mineral plan. According to Dr. Ronald Thompson, Director, Vitamin and Supplement Research and Development of General Nutrition Inc., it is possible that Vitamin C, Vitamin A (beta-Carotene is a smarter choice since it carries no risk of Vitamin A toxicity) and Zinc requirements are increased after you stop smoking. These nutrients, especially, are needed for wound healing. Vitamin A is needed for epithelial-cell production and maintenance of mucosal membranes in lungs.

I also recommend the following: Vitamin B1 (thiamine) and B5 (pantothenic acid) give a calming effect. Vitamin B6 (pyridoxine) is a safe diuretic that helps with the stiffness of hands, feet and fingers. Vitamin E can combine with pollutants and render them harmless. Calcium eases excess stress.

To get the full benefit from your vitamins and minerals, I recommend "natural" vitamins. Take them with food to potentiate the vitamin and protect the lining of your stomach.

SETTING UP A SUPPORT SYSTEM

Quitting with a buddy, or having a special person or persons support you while you quit smoking, can make a big difference to your morale and success. Then again, you may prefer to quit alone and be left alone. How you decide to proceed is a personal decision. Here are three options for setting up a support system:

1) Buddy System— Quitting with a buddy can be a great idea and lots of fun, but only if he or she is as serious about quitting smoking as you are. If you have a Stop-Smoking Buddy in mind, you should schedule your sessions at the same times and counsel each other through parts of the program.

● Quit together and meet with each other for your scheduled appointments. Take turns counseling each other through the counter-conditioning part of the program.

● Make plans to spend time together. See a movie, play some tennis, go out for dinner, or just spend a quiet evening together.

● Set up a hot-line with each other. Make an agreement that before lighting up a cigarette, you will phone and get support. Sometimes, just the act of picking up the phone and keeping your commitment to make the call is all that's needed to prevent you from lighting up. If your buddy is not home, don't use it as an excuse to smoke. Call someone else, or do something else.

Name of Buddy _____

Work # _____

Home # _____

Best Times

To Call _____

It's easiest to quit smoking with another quitter. A little ego and competition between the two of you can add incentive.

2) Support of Family and Friends— If you don't have a Stop-Smoking Buddy, or don't like the idea of quitting with someone, there is an alternative. Inform friends, family, or other significant people in your life about your decision to quit. Then enlist their cooperation and support if and when you need it.

● If you live with family or friends, ask those around you to be particularly cooperative and understanding during "Kick It" Week. If they know what makes you angry, ask them in advance not to provoke you. Let them know that you may be more irritable than usual when you quit, and that this is a symptom of nicotine withdrawal. Remind them not to take your short temper personally. You may prefer more time alone, or you may want to have them around for company. Let your needs be known.

● If they're willing, ask them to participate in special treats. They can make life easier for you by making dinner, taking you out for dinner, planning a picnic, or taking care of your errands and housework.

● Set up a hot line. Make an agreement with another supportive person, or persons, that before lighting up a cigarette, you will call them for support.

Name of Supportive Persons _____

_____

_____

Work # _____

Home # _____

Best Times
To Call _____

3) Quitting Alone—If you're alone, or prefer to quit in private, here are some ideas for creating your own support system:

● Make "Kick It" Week easier by taking care of unpleasant tasks in advance. Do shopping and cleaning the day or two *before* you quit.

● Reward yourself with your favorite hobbies, meals, and relaxing activities.

● Set up a hot-line by choosing an emotionally uninvolved person like a counselor, priest or rabbi to support you through quitting. If you feel silly about getting them involved, look at it this way: Wouldn't you rather get their support to help you live longer, than keep smoking because you're too embarrassed to ask for their help?

● Free psychological counseling centers, the American Cancer Society, or The American Lung Association provide free information about kicking the smoking habit. Also check the listing in your phone book under *Smoker's Information and Treatment Center*. Call them and get their support.

American Cancer Society # _____

American Lung Association # _____

Smoker's Information and

Treatment Center # _____

Counselor # _____

Other # _____

It doesn't matter who you call or what they say. It's often the act of picking up the phone and breaking the pattern of reaching for a cigarette that will prevent you from relapsing.

Susan, a former pack-a-day smoker and client of mine, invented a unique hot-line system: Every time she had an impulse to smoke a cigarette, she called the recorded time message. As she sat and listened to the seconds and minutes tick by, she was reminded that life is too short. She didn't want to cut into the quality and quantity of time she has left to her life. Needless to say, her urge to smoke disappeared quickly.

HOW TO SMOKE YOUR LAST FEW CIGARETTES BEFORE "KICK IT" WEEK

Before you panic, thinking that today is the last day you can smoke, I want to remind you that you will be smoking in the course of the first three days of the program. However the kind of smoking in your Stop-Smoking sessions will be different than what you are normally used to. Starting tomorrow, you will be smoking to "turn off" to cigarettes by going through a process technically called *counter-conditioning*.

Counter-conditioning is a fancy term for *re-learning* your conditioned thoughts, feelings and actions regarding smoking. Just as you've learned to enjoy smoking long enough to become addicted to nicotine, you can unlearn that response. You can counteract the circumstances that trapped you into the habit in the first place. Tomorrow you will start the counter-conditioning exercises and start "turning off" to smoking.

In the meantime, start by taking a close look at what it is about cigarettes you enjoy. And, on the other end of the spectrum, look at what already turns you off to smoking.

As you smoke today and tomorrow—until you begin your first day's session—keep your senses open and sharpened to the smoking experience. Taste that cigarette. Smell it. Feel the smoke in your throat and chest.

Notice your body posture as you hold your cigarette. Notice your facial expression as you take a drag. Look for new sensations that perhaps you weren't experiencing before, and ask yourself: "What do I love about this cigarette? Do I like the taste, the smell, the feeling in my chest, the buzz from the drug, the sense of comfort I get from holding it, or sucking on it? Do I like watching the smoke entering and exiting my body? Do I like flicking ashes, lighting the lighter or matches?

What is 'turning me on' or 'turning me off' to smoking?"

RECORD YOUR FEELINGS ABOUT SMOKING IN THE SPACE BELOW. YOU WILL NEED THIS INFORMATION FOR TOMORROW'S SESSION:

Smoking's "Turn Ons"

_____
_____
_____
_____
_____
_____

Smoking's "Turn Offs"

_____
_____
_____
_____
_____
_____

Continue to smoke and observe your feelings about it until tomorrow's session, when you will be given further instructions on how to proceed.

A LAST WORD
BEFORE YOU QUIT TOMORROW

Tomorrow you are going to quit smoking. You're not going to try to quit. You're not going to give it your best shot. You're going to make up your mind *now* that you will be successful for the first 24 hours of the program. What I'm driving at is this: Trying doesn't work! Only doing works!

You're already familiar with the addict and how it operates. You've learned to cope with the many thoughts and behaviors that can get in the way of success. You're mentally and physically prepared for the big day.

But I've been saving the most important information about the addict for today so that this information will be fresh in your mind when you quit tomorrow.

ONE PUFF ON A CIGARETTE WILL READDICT YOU TO SMOKING!

When you're dealing with addiction, you can't leave any room for failure. When you "try," you imply that you can fail. When you "Give it your best shot," you're saying it's possible that your best won't be good enough.

IF YOU GIVE THE ADDICT AN INCH OF OPPORTUNITY TO SMOKE, IT TAKES A MILE. IN NO TIME YOU'LL BE SMOKING FULL FORCE AGAIN.

The addict responds only to absolutes—quitting 100% or not quitting at all. It takes a lot of guts to put yourself on the line and make a 100% commitment to this. But that's what it takes to break this habit once and for all.

Relax, and make an absolute commitment now. I'll give you the tools and show you how to use them to make it through. You will succeed . . . one day at a time. Big changes happen when you commit to them totally. The rest is easy. Follow through step by step.

SUPPLIES FOR TOMORROW

For tomorrow's session, you will need one pack of your favorite brand of cigarettes, a large glass jar filled with about two inches of water and a lighter or matches.

IMPORTANT INFORMATION AND ADVICE

In the course of Days 1 through 3, you will be asked to do some rapid smoking. You will be inhaling no more than one cigarette every seven seconds. And you'll be puffing—not fully inhaling—on no more than four cigarettes per session. This method has been used effectively at the Habit Breakers Clinic for more than five years to help smokers kick the habit and lose the desire to resume.

Individuals susceptible to or with a history of stroke, heart attack, emphysema, dizzy spells, hyperglycemia or hypoglycemia, or pregnant women shouldn't participate in the rapid-inhalation-of-smoke exercise. I've provided you with an alternative treatment for that particular exercise.

If you feel ill or faint during any part of this program, please stop the exercise!

If you have any questions regarding your full participation in the counter-conditioning exercises, please consult your physician first.

Day 1: Withdrawing From Nicotine & Turning Off To Smoking

PLEASE HAVE READY YOUR CIGARETTES, LIGHTER OR MATCHES, AND A LARGE GLASS JAR WITH TWO INCHES OF WATER IN IT. DO NOT SMOKE UNTIL YOU ARE TOLD TO DO SO, WHICH WILL BE JUST AFTER YOU READ THE FOLLOWING SECTION.

HOW TO HANDLE NICOTINE WITHDRAWAL

Today you are going to quit smoking. By the time you complete this section, you will know how to handle your cravings for tobacco. In the next few days you will be free of nicotine, so relax. You'll be

OK without your cigarettes when you put them out today for the next 24 hours.

First, let's look at the most commonly asked questions about nicotine withdrawal:

Q: What are the symptoms of withdrawal?
A: About 90% of all quitters experience some of the following symptoms although few experience all of them:

- Craving for tobacco
- Dizziness, spaciness, inability to concentrate
- Irritability and anger
- Anxiety
- Sleepiness and lack of energy
- Restlessness
- Headaches
- Coughing
- Mouth sores and skin odors
- Hunger
- Constipation
- Dreaming that you've smoked

These are the worst symptoms you can expect from quitting, and after this session, you'll know how to take care of them.

Q: How long do these symptoms last?
A: Fortunately, only about 72 hours. These symptoms will subside after that. However, I have seen some quitters go through withdrawal in 24 hours. And I've seen it take longer than 72 hours. Every-

one responds differently. The most important thing to know is that these withdrawal symptoms are temporary. They are a small price to pay for breaking a habit that is destroying your body daily.

Here's a graph of what the typical "Kick It" Week looks like in terms of your craving for tobacco:

NICOTINE WITHDRAWAL

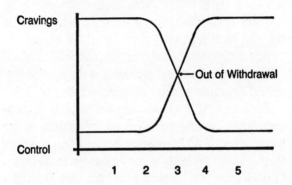

At Day 1 your craving for tobacco is high, and your control is low. By Day 4 you will begin to experience relief from the withdrawal symptoms. And by the time nicotine leaves your system, this craving will decrease. Again, it may take longer or shorter than 72 hours, depending on your body's reaction to withdrawal.

Q: Why do these symptoms occur, and what can I do to ease them?

A: They occur because your body is going through a major chemical change. Fortunately, there's quite a bit you can do to ease the discomfort.

Craving for Tobacco—You crave tobacco because the nicotine in it is an addictive drug that has you chemically hooked to smoking. You need this drug much like a heroin addict needs a "fix." If you smoke a pack a day, you need a fix every 20 minutes or so. Breathing is the only thing that you do with such regularity.

According to a government pamphlet entitled "Why People Smoke," smoking is the most widespread example of drug dependence in the U.S.

Because you're chemically dependent on nicotine, your craving for tobacco intensifies as the bloodstream level of nicotine begins to drop. When this happens, the body sends a message to the brain: "I need nicotine," which translates into "I need a cigarette." Even if you've never quit before, you must be familiar with the discomfort and irritability, such as when you run out of cigarettes for the night and all the stores are closed. *That's* the feeling.

Here are some things to do that will rid your body of nicotine and speed up the withdrawal process:

● Drink plenty of water and fluids. The more you urinate, the faster the body cleanses itself. A good guideline is six to eight glasses of water a day.

● Exercise and sweat out the toxins. The more you sweat, the more your body can eliminate nicotine through the pores of the skin.

● Take a hot bath, sauna, or jacuzzi. This opens up your pores and allows you to eliminate nicotine faster.

● Avoid red meat. Red meat may make the body retain nicotine.

Dizziness, Spaciness and Inability to Concentrate—If you find that you can't balance your checkbook, or carry on a conversation, it's because your body chemistry is readjusting to a drop in the bloodstream's nicotine level.

The other reason for these symptoms is that you inhale carbon monoxide (CO) when you smoke. CO robs your body of oxygen and leaves your brain oxygen-starved. When you quit smoking, your brain receives a lot more oxygen than you're used to, so you may get lightheaded.

There isn't much you can do about these symptoms. Let them run their course. If you get a little dizzy, common sense will tell you to lie down and take it easy. If you find that you can't concentrate, or can't get your work done, have a little patience with yourself. This feeling will pass very soon.

In the mean time, exercise. Exercising will improve your circulation and subsequently improve your ability to concentrate.

Irritability and Anger—If you feel irritable or

angry during withdrawal, it's understandable. Don't forget that by giving up smoking, you're putting yourself through a major psychological as well as chemical change. Have a little patience with your short temper and remind those around you to be more tolerant of any mood changes. The best thing you can do about this irritability is to laugh at yourself. Remember, you once used cigarettes to suck down your anger and aggravation. Now that you don't use cigarettes anymore, you will need to learn to cope with anger and aggravation more constructively:

● Get physical! Exercise, jogging, dancing, or stretching can help get your frustrations out and leave you feeling good about yourself.

● If you feel rage, punch a pillow or yell—in the bathroom or in your car with the windows rolled up—or kick a ball. It can temporarily calm you down.

● If you don't want to get physical, or if you can't under the circumstances, talk out your feelings with a friend, write them down on paper, or cry them out for relief.

● Use effective communication. Some quitters complain that they are horrible to be around when quitting. If you want to remain your usual, nice self, despite the changes you're going through, avoid blaming, criticizing, name-calling, judging, or being sarcastic.

Express your feelings by using "I" messages instead of "You" messages. For example, instead of saying "You did this assignment all wrong" say "I would appreciate it if you made the following corrections on this assignment." Using "I" avoids arousing defenses in the other person and makes your life easier by avoiding arguments.

Stay in the present. Don't bring up arguments or events from the past. If you're angry because your soup is cold, don't bring up all the times you've had to eat cold soup. In a nutshell, think of the consequences of what you say and how you say it before you speak.

Anxiety—Giving up a psychological crutch and experiencing withdrawal symptoms can make you anxious. Keep recognizing the huge changes you're undergoing this week. Don't forget that smoking is so embedded in every aspect of your life that quitting can make you feel like your world is caving in.

In the mean time, eat right, take your vitamins, and be sure you're getting plenty of calcium. Calcium helps the body calm down. Milk, cheese, cottage cheese, yogurt and any dairy product or calcium supplements will provide you with this mineral.

Sleepiness or Lack of Energy—You may feel sleepy and lack energy because you're withdrawing from a stimulant. As a smoker, you were constantly pumping yourself up with an energizer, or slowing yourself down with a depressant—nicotine has a paradoxical effect.

ENERGY CURVE

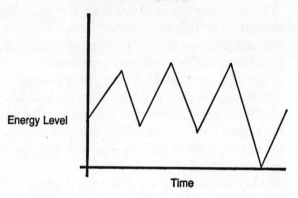

Energy Level

Time

When you got up in the morning, one of the first things you may have done was light up a cigarette. That first cigarette had some powerful effects on your central nervous system. Nicotine stimulates the central nervous system and the adrenal glands, boosting your energy. Have you ever had the feeling that you just can't get going in the morning without your cigarettes? And you may have needed coffee too! The reason you can't get it together without your stimulant is that your system is hooked on operating with it.

But the problem with a nicotine stimulant is that 20 minutes later nicotine has a depressant effect, causing you to need another pick-me-up, another cigarette. And so the vicious cycle continues.

This energy rise and fall stresses your body. It can leave you feeling dragged down, tired, and stressed by the end of the day.

When you quit tomorrow, you will stop relying on cigarettes for that characteristic energy lift. Therefore, you'll need to rely on good nutrition and exercise instead.

Restlessness—If you find that you're restless and can't sit still, remember that cigarettes played a major role in keeping boredom away. If you feel restless before going to sleep, a few calcium tablets, a hot glass of milk, some herb tea or a hot bath should take care of it.

Headaches—Occasionally, quitters get headaches. Withdrawal from nicotine takes a toll in many ways. It's a poisonous drug that has been affecting your nervous system. The headaches will pass shortly.

Coughing—Quitters oftentime complain that they cough more after quitting than when they smoked. Coughing is a sign of cleansing. Your bronchial cilia, hairlike structures along the bronchial passageway, are busy lifting tar and dirt from your lungs. These cilia have been paralyzed by smoke. The smoker's cough is, in fact, trying to do the work that the cilia used to do. When you quit smoking, they start doing their own work again. To help sooth the irritation, drink herb tea.

Mouth Sores and Skin Odors—These are not very common withdrawal symptoms. The reason for them is that the body is ridding itself of smoking's poisons. Sometimes cleansing can mean sores or bad odors. Be happy that you're body has this great capacity to rid itself of poisons.

Hunger—Quitting smoking doesn't necessarily mean gaining weight. Because you're withdrawing from a stimulant, your metabolism decreases slightly and slows your ability to burn fat. This accounts for no more than two to three excess pounds in the first couple of months. Any more than that is an indication that you've substituted food for cigarettes. Here are alternatives:

● Eat light, nutritious meals.

● Don't skip meals.

● Eat low-calorie snacks or use oral substitutes to satisfy your need for oral gratification and curb your appetite.

Constipation—Without the stimulant nicotine, your bowels may slow its function. If you find that you have trouble with constipation, here are some suggestions:

● Eat a high-fiber diet. Fruits, grains, nuts, vegetables are high in fiber and help pass food through the intestines.

● Drink plenty of fluids to improve the bowels' functioning. I personally think that drinking hot liquids speeds up the process.

● And of course, prunes or prune juice work.

It won't be long before your body gets accustomed to functioning without nicotine. If any of the above symptoms concern or pain you, please consult your physician.

Dreaming That You've Smoked—Dreaming about smoking is very common. Quitters often dream that they've smoked a cigarette and are re-addicted to smoking. For many, the dream is so real that they feel guilty when they awaken. Dreaming that you've smoked is your way of working out the loss of smoking. This symptom can persist weeks after quitting. Have fun smoking in your dreams. It's the safest cigarette you can smoke.

EATING FOR ENERGY

The best way to counteract the stress of withdrawal symptoms and the energy rise and fall is to refocus your attention on good nutrition and exercise while noting all the changes and benefits.

● Eat a high-protein breakfast. You'll need something to sustain you through the morning. Good sources of protein are beans, cheese, milk, eggs, fish, chicken, and soy products such as tofu.

● Try the *Habit-Breakers Quickie Breakfast*. Many clients say they hate eating in the morning. They'd rather skip breakfast than stomach food. I say, if you can't *eat* your breakfast, *drink* your breakfast. *Mix one cup of non-fat or low-fat milk with a half banana and an egg in the blender at high speed for 20 seconds*. If you prefer, try different juices for variety, instead of milk. If you don't eat eggs, add protein powder instead. You can put in any type of fruit—try it with raspberries or blueberries.

● If you need a pick-me-up during the day, try a piece of fruit, some whole-grain bread or cereal, or a glass of juice. Carbohydrates are instant-fuel foods.

● Don't skip meals. You don't want to let your energy drop. Three meals are recommended, but you may want to have five smaller meals instead.

● Don't forget to take your vitamins and minerals.

● I recommend that you avoid the following substances because they also throw your blood-sugar level off kilter and actually set you up for an energy plunge: coffee, caffeinated tea, alcohol, sugar and any stimulant except those you must take by prescription. They will trigger your need for a cigarette.

YOUR CURRENT ASSOCIATIONS WITH SMOKING

Remember your first cigarette? Remember the coughing, the dizziness, the nausea? You worked hard to train yourself to enjoy smoking. Now it's time to work hard to train yourself to dislike it.

Today you will begin the process of unraveling your many positive associations with smoking, and start replacing them with negative ones. Let me explain how this works.

SOME OF YOUR CURRENT ASSOCIATIONS WITH SMOKING ARE BACK ON PAGE 49. RECORD THEM BELOW AGAIN.

Positive Associations: "Turn Ons"

_____
_____
_____
_____
_____
_____

Negative Associations: "Turn Offs"

_____
_____
_____
_____
_____
_____

When you think of a cigarette, you may also think "refreshing, relaxing, rewarding" because these are the aspects of smoking you've focused on to continue the habit.

But what if you forced yourself to focus on the negative aspects of smoking—the bad, bitter taste, the coughing and congestion, and the stale smell of tobacco on your body and breath? Eventually, your desire for smoking would leave. Today you're going to learn to "turn off" to tobacco by *re-experiencing* smoking in a negative way.

I want to emphasize the word *experience* because "talk therapy" doesn't work. You can't be talked out of a habit. If you could, all you'd need are a few good reasons for quitting and you'd quit. You've tried that already with no success, haven't you?

Habits don't respond to "talk therapy," but they do respond to images and sensory stimulation. Because of this, even the strongest habits can be broken if they are sensorally re-experienced in a negative way. And this is how you are going to break the smoking habit.

IF YOU ARE PREGNANT, OR SUSPECT THAT YOU ARE, IF YOU HAVE HEART PROBLEMS, HIGH BLOOD PRESSURE, HYPERGLYCEMIA OR HYPOGLYCEMIA, EMPHYSEMA, OR IF YOU HAVE HAD A STROKE, PLEASE DO NOT INHALE MORE THAN TWO CIGARETTES DURING THE COURSE OF THIS SESSION.

PROCEED SLOWLY WITH THE EXERCISE TO AVOID RAPID INHALATION OF SMOKE THAT CAN CAUSE DIZZINESS, HEART PALPITATIONS, AND FAINTING SPELLS.

IF YOU FEEL LIGHTHEADED, OR SICK DURING THE COUNTER-CONDITIONING EXERCISE, STOP IMMEDIATELY!

IF YOU HAVE ANY QUESTIONS OR CONCERNS ABOUT THE COUNTER-CONDITIONING EXERCISES, CONSULT YOUR PHYSICIAN FIRST.

COUNTER-CONDITIONING SESSION: TURNING OFF TO SMOKING

OK, it's time to smoke. Buddies, here is where you can take turns coaching each other how to smoke. First Buddy, read the instructions to your partner starting here:

- "Open your pack of cigarettes, take one out, and light up."
- "Inhale. Take a few seconds to think about what is enjoyable about that puff."

WRITE DOWN THE THREE MOST ENJOYABLE ASPECTS OF THAT FIRST PUFF:

_____

_____

_____

● "Take another 'drag.' Think. What else do you enjoy about smoking? Circle the ones that apply to you: Taste, smell, warmth, smoke, sucking motion, holding, feeling in chest, or the high from the drug."

● "For the next 10 puffs you're going to pretend that your body has developed an allergy to smoke. Before you inhale your next puff, I want you to imagine the sooty, tarry smoke going down into your chest and cutting off your oxygen supply. Imagine that you're suffocating from smoke and you can barely breathe. Got the feeling? OK, proceed:"

10) "Inhale and cough up the smoke. Your mouth is beginning to taste bitter."

9) "Inhale and cough it up again. The bitter flavor is getting stronger and your throat feels dry and scratchy."

8) "Inhale and cough. Your throat feels tight and dry, and your chest feels congested."

7) "Inhale and cough. Picture the heavy, tarry smoke sitting in your chest, pressing down on you like a ton of bricks."

6) "Inhale and cough. Your chest feels tight, and you're having trouble breathing."

5) "Inhale and cough. Your chest feels congested and you can hardly breathe."

4) "Inhale and cough. You can feel a tight lump at the back of your throat and your lungs feel raw and irritated."

3) "Inhale and cough. Your throat feels raw; your chest feels heavy; and you can barely squeeze the smoke down into your chest."

2) "Inhale and cough it up—*hard.*"

1) "Inhale and cough it up again—*harder!*"

● "Are you ready to put this cigarette out? Get out your jar full of water, and throw your cigarette butt in the jar."

Second Buddy, please switch roles with your partner and have him or her instruct you through the last exercise.

FANTASY SMOKING

In just a few minutes, I'm going to teach you a very satisfying technique called *Fantasy Smoking*. This is just what it implies: You're going to learn to create a feeling of pleasure and relaxation from an imaginary cigarette. You're actually going to learn how you can have your cake—go through the pleasurable motions of smoking—and eat it too—not pay the negative consequences.

Since this is an imaginary cigarette, you can make it as wonderful as you want. You may want to pretend that you're inhaling a cool, minty white cloud—if you like mentholated cigarettes. If you prefer a warm feeling in your chest, you may want to imagine inhaling the fresh warm air on a desert walk. It's *your* Fantasy Cigarette—it can taste and feel any way you want it to.

While you are smoking your Fantasy Cigarette, you're also going to smoke a real one. As a matter of fact, you will be going back and forth between inhaling the Fantasy Cigarette, and the real one as you rate each inhalation in terms of the pleasure you're getting.

As you inhale the real cigarette, look for the "turn offs" about smoking. This shouldn't be too hard to do after that last cigarette. The Fantasy Cigarette goes in the hand that you normally hold your cigarette with. The real cigarette goes in the opposite hand. You may want to use a coffee stirrer, a cinnamon stick or a straw to make the Fantasy Cigarette feel more real. So go get one if you wish, although using nothing at all works just as well.

BEFORE YOU BEGIN THE FANTASY SMOKING EXERCISE, PLEASE READ THROUGH IT FIRST. BUDDIES, READ THE FOLLOWING EXERCISE TO YOUR

PARTNER AND CHANGE ROLES WHEN YOU'RE DONE.

● Ready for your next cigarette? Good. Light one up; switch it to your non-smoking hand; and hold that Fantasy Cigarette in your smoking one. When you have all of this figured out, start switching back and forth.

● First inhale the Fantasy Cigarette. Mentally rate it in terms of it's pleasure on a 1 to 10 scale— 10 being fantastic and 1 being horrible. Then do the same with the real cigarette. Rate each inhalation for the next 10 puffs. If the real cigarette tastes better than the Fantasy Cigarette after 10 puffs, you're not concentrating hard enough on the "turn off" feelings about smoking. STOP after 10 puffs.

● Coaching Buddy, continue coaching until the end of the exercise. Ready for your last real cigarette of the day? OK, light up. Inhale throughout the entire exercise as you repeat to yourself while Buddy reads the following messages:

10) Inhale. "Smoking irritates my throat."

9) Inhale. "Smoking irritates my eyes."

8) Inhale. "Smoking leaves me with a bitter taste in my mouth."

7) Inhale. "Smoking burns my lips and tongue."

6) Inhale. "Smoking coats my lungs, teeth and body with tar."

5) Inhale and cough it up. "Smoking leaves me short of breath."

4) Inhale and cough. "Smoking leaves my throat feeling dry and scratchy."

3) Inhale and cough again. "Smoking leaves my chest feeling heavy and congested."

2) Inhale and cough again. "Smoking leaves my chest feeling tight and congested, and I can't breathe."

1) Inhale and cough it up *hard* and say to yourself: "Cigarettes are beginning to lose some of their power over me. It's perfectly OK with me to put them out for the next 24 hours."

Good. Put out your cigarette in the jar of water.

IF YOU STILL HAVE THE URGE TO SMOKE, REPEAT THE LAST EXERCISE. IF YOU HAVE MEDICAL PROBLEMS, AND STILL HAVE THE URGE TO SMOKE, LIGHT UP ANOTHER CIGARETTE, INHALE AND COUGH UP THE SMOKE THREE MORE TIMES, AND STOP THE EXERCISE!

CLEARING THE AIR

Put the smoked butts in your jar of water, take the remaining cigarettes out of the pack, break them in half, and flush them down the toilet.

Keep the jar in a conspicuous place, such as on your desk, so you can be reminded of the look and smell of the smoking habit. Whenever you have an urge to smoke, open the jar and take a whiff of that "delicious" aroma.

Check your drawers, pant and jacket pockets, your purse, and all the places you usually keep cigarettes. Flush those you find down the toilet too. Many a desperate quitter has readdicted him or herself by fishing a cigarette butt out of the garbage can.

Brush your teeth, have a cold glass of water, and join me back here when you're done.

HANDLING YOUR URGE TO SMOKE

When withdrawing from nicotine, you may experience some intense cravings to smoke. Here are some methods to help you cope:

Pseudo-Lamaze—The first technique you're about to learn is an adaptation of the Lamaze method for pain control that pregnant women have used for years to ease the pain of childbirth. I've given birth to two children using this technique, and if it works to ease the pain of labor, it works equally well to ease the discomfort of tobacco cravings.

You will need a comfortable place to sit or lie down. Then choose a *focal point*. A focal point is simply an object that's comfortably above eye level. Shiny, or bright objects are good focal points, as long as they're not too bright and don't hurt your eyes.

You have your focal point now. When that urge to smoke hits, take a deep breath in through your nose, letting that breath travel all the way up to the top of your head, and exhale through your mouth. If you're uncomfortable breathing nasally, breathe through your mouth instead. As you breathe in, say to yourself, "Hello urge. I knew you'd be around sooner or later. I'm going to blow you away with this breathing technique."

As you concentrate on your focal point, continue breathing deeply—in through your nose, and out your mouth—as you project your discomfort onto your focal point. Pretend that your urge to smoke is out there, instead of inside of you. With each exhalation, you will blow this urge farther and farther out into space, until it disappears.

When the urge is gone, take another deep breath. Blow it out as you say to yourself, "Goodbye urge. I feel powerful knowing that I can control my desire for a cigarette without lighting one up."

OK, now try it. Get comfortable with this technique before you need to use it.

Alternative Breathing Technique—Here's an alternative method for when you're not alone and can't take time out to do the "pseudo-Lamaze" method.

When the craving for tobacco hits, take a deep breath in through your nose, all the way to the top of your head. Then exhale this craving out of your body, through the souls of your feet, and down into the ground. Use the breath to ground the static build-up of tension caused by cravings for tobacco. Now practice it.

If you don't remember any of these techniques when you need them most, take slow, deep breaths.

From what you can already see, you're going to be doing a lot of deep breathing today. Don't forget that a large part of the pleasure of smoking has to do with taking deep inhalations.

You see, smoking was really the only time you breathed deeply and let out the stress built up during the day. Now that you're not smoking, you'll have to constantly remind yourself to do this. Fortunately, you're only giving up smoking—you needn't give up breathing.

SENSE MEMORY EXERCISE

Sense Memory is a way of recreating the memory of past emotional experiences and physical sensations. Actors use this technique all the time to give a more genuine performance. If you were an actor and had to play a sad scene, you would act more authentically if you could remember in great detail an unhappy incident in your life to recreate the feeling of sadness.

Starting today, you're going to use your Sense Memory to recreate the memory of today's session to "turn off" to smoking. When the urge hits, you are going to recall the heat, congestion, bitterness, and irritation you experienced in today's smoking session. Try this *now* while the experience is still fresh in your mind.

LIST HERE THE THREE MOST PROMINENT "TURN OFFS" YOU EXPERIENCED IN TODAY'S SESSION:

_____

_____

_____

READ THE FOLLOWING EXERCISE FIRST BEFORE YOU TRY IT.

Close your eyes and pretend that you're lighting up a cigarette. Inhale and cough it up. Now flood your memory with the three most prominent "turn off" sensations you felt during today's session, one sensation at a time. Feel the smoke in your mouth and in your chest. Smell the smoke curling up your nostrils.

Let these sensations register on a gut level. You'll know you've got it on a gut level when you actually feel these "turn off" sensations you're re-creating.

When you have an urge to smoke, all you need to do is recall these feelings and watch your urge to smoke disappear.

Here's the point I'm making: Don't flirt with your desire for a cigarette. If you find yourself focusing on smoking's "turn ons," stop that train of thought and use your Sense Memory to counteract it with "turn off" sensations.

The more you practice this Sense Memory exercise, the more effective you will be at eliminating your urge to smoke. Practice your Sense Memory at least 20 times today.

I've given you a lot of material to absorb. At the back of the book on page 148, you will see a section entitled *Quitter's Survival Guide*. Everything you need to know to quit smoking successfully is in it. You will also find a *Deep Relaxation Exercise* on page 142. Use it to help you fall asleep tonight.

TOMORROW'S SUPPLIES

For tomorrow's session, you will need one pack of your least favorite brand of cigarettes, a large glass jar filled with two inches of water, a lighter or matches and a watch or clock with a "seconds" hand.

DON'T BUY YOUR CIGARETTES UNTIL RIGHT BEFORE YOUR SESSION. DON'T OPEN THEM UNTIL YOU'RE INSTRUCTED TO DO SO, OR YOU WILL READDICT YOURSELF!

You're well on your way to changing your relationship with your smoking habit and breaking free from cigarettes. Let me remind you again: *One puff on a cigarette—other than the smoking you are instructed to do during the program—has the power to readdict you!*

TAKE THE NEXT FEW MINUTES TO SIGN A CONTRACT WITH YOURSELF TO STOP SMOKING FOR THE NEXT 24 HOURS.

24-HOUR CONTRACT TO QUIT SMOKING

I, _____ commit to quitting smoking for the next 24 hours.

I've rid my environment of cigarettes, and will not purchase any until directly before my next session. I will not open this purchased pack until instructed to do so.

I will use the techniques I've learned in this last session to cope with the next 24 hours without a cigarette.

LOOK THROUGH YOUR 3X5 CARDS. FIND AND LIST THE FIVE MOST IMPORTANT BENEFITS YOU GET FROM QUITTING SMOKING, AND THE FIVE MOST IMPORTANT CONSEQUENCES YOU INCUR AS A SMOKER.

I am quitting smoking for myself, and of my own free will and I'm choosing to do so for the following reasons:

Benefits of Quitting

_____

_____

_____

_____

_____

Consequences of Smoking

_____

_____

_____

_____

_____

Signed _____

Date _____

Congratulations, ex-smoker. See you tomorrow at the same time.

Day 2: Transforming Your Relationship With Smoking

DON'T OPEN YOUR PACK OF CIGARETTES UNTIL YOU ARE INSTRUCTED TO SMOKE. IT'S VITAL TO THE SUCCESS OF THE PROGRAM THAT YOU WAIT.

Congratulations, ex-smoker! You made it throught the first 24 hours without a cigarette. But now you're anxious to smoke those cigarettes you just picked up from the store. Most quitters are. In just a few minutes, you'll have a chance to smoke them.

Yesterday, I talked about the positive associations you build up with smoking. Let's take a closer look at how the mind decides that—"Smoking is relaxing." The best puff on a cigarette is the first one, according to most quitters in the Habit-Breakers program. This is because it takes a few seconds for nicotine to do its work. You're actually getting oxygen with the first drag, and it leaves you with the false association that smoking is relaxing because the nicotine is not yet affecting you.

It's only after the cigarette is out that you begin to feel uncomfortable—eyes burn, nasal passage dried out, chest tight. You make another false association—"not smoking is irritating." The mind never makes the connection that smoking causes the discomfort in the first place because there is no direct connection between the irritation and the cigarette. The cigarette is already out by the time the irritation sets in! So you end up with two false equations:

Smoking = Relaxation, and Not Smoking = Irritation.

Today you're going to turn your relationship with smoking 180 degrees, and reverse these equations by allowing your body to directly experience the smoking-induced irritation.

Because you haven't smoked for 24 hours, you are extremely sensitive to nicotine. Today, when you smoke, you're going to experience how the drug is *killing you!*

PHYSIOLOGICAL EFFECTS OF SMOKING

You will soon be asked to inhale a cigarette every seven seconds. This is what will happen:

● Your heart rate will increase because smoking stimulates certain glands to release adrenalin and powerful hormones. This causes the walls of the heart to contract more strongly and more often. This increases the heart rate and the heart's need for oxygen and nutrients.

● Your blood vessels will strongly constrict, increasing your blood pressure, interfering with blood flow to the limbs and leaving you with a tingly feeling in your fingers and toes.

● Your oxygen supply will decrease. Carbon monoxide makes up about 4% of a cigarette's smoke and has a stronger affinity, or attraction to red blood cells than does oxygen. Red blood cells distribute oxygen throughout the body. This 4% of CO in the red blood cells quickly robs the bloodstream of it's oxygen supply, thus impairing vision, judgment, attention to sound, and athletic performance. It also makes you feel dizzy and spacey, and interferes with your ability to think clearly.

● You may feel slightly nauseous and sweaty because of the presence of nicotine in your bloodstream. Smoking reduces your stomach's ability to buffer stomach acid. Your body responds to nicotine by retarding the stomach buffers causing acid stomach. Imagine what 20 cigarettes a day does to your stomach lining. That's why so many smokers live with painful ulcers.

RESTING PULSE

Before you start smoking, take your resting

pulse. Find a good strong pulse spot on your wrist. Take your pulse for 10 seconds, and then multiply this number by 6 to get the number of heartbeats per minute. For example, if you get a count of 12 beats per 10 seconds, your resting pulse is calculated by multiplying 12x6, which equals 72 beats per minute.

$$\underline{\hspace{3cm}} \times 6 = \underline{\hspace{3cm}}$$

Number of beats   x 6 =   Your resting pulse
per 10 seconds

COUNTER-CONDITIONING SESSION

The rapid inhalation of smoke you will be instructed to do during this exercise is a very effective tool to help you break your positive associations with smoking. But it may be bad for you.

IF YOU HAVE MEDICAL PROBLEMS, IF YOU ARE PREGNANT, OR SUSPECT THAT YOU ARE, IF YOU HAVE HEART PROBLEMS, HIGH BLOOD PRESSURE, HYPERGLYCEMIA OR HYPOGLYCEMIA, EMPHYSEMA, OR IF YOU HAVE HAD A STROKE, PLEASE DO THE ALTERNATIVE COUNTER-CONDITIONING EXERCISE ON PAGE 86.

THE REST OF YOU: DO NOT SMOKE MORE THAN ONE CIGARETTE DURING THE RAPID-INHALATION PART OF THIS EXERCISE.

If you feel lightheaded, or sick during the counter-conditioning exercise, stop immediately!

Consult your physician before participating in the rapid inhalation part of this exercise.

READ THE ENTIRE EXERCISE FIRST BEFORE SMOKING.

Rapid Inhalation of Smoke—For the duration of one cigarette, you will inhale every seven seconds as you look for the effects of increased heartrate, tingliness in the extremities, spaciness, dizziness, nausea and acid stomach.

Stop smoking as soon as you feel some of these physiological effects. If you feel faint, or ill, stop the exercise immediately. Even if you don't feel any of these effects, stop the exercise anyway. Continue with the alternate counter-conditioning exercise.

Take out a cigarette, break off the filter, light up, and start inhaling every seven seconds. Work as you choose, alone, or with a Buddy. Do and say the following:

10) Inhale and cough it up. "I'm poisoning my body with nicotine."

9) Inhale. "The nicotine has hit my brain, and I feel the effects of the drug."

8) Inhale. "My head feels dizzy from the lack of oxygen."

7) Inhale. "I feel lightheaded and drugged."

6) Inhale. "My heart is starting to beat harder and faster."

5) Inhale. "I can feel some tingliness in my fingers and toes."

4) Inhale. "I feel spacey and my thinking is unclear."

3) Inhale. "My stomach feels a little queasy."

2) Inhale. "I'm starting to feel a bit nauseous from the drug."

1) Inhale and cough it up *hard*. "Cigarettes are beginning to lose some of their power over me."

TAKE YOUR PULSE RATE AGAIN, AND RECORD IT HERE: _____

NOW TAKE YOUR RESTING PULSE RATE, AND SUBTRACT IT FROM THIS NUMBER.

_____ − _____ = _____
Resting pulse   Pulse after   Difference
                 smoking

To get the percentage increased pulse rate after smoking, take the difference between the two rates and divide it by your resting pulse.

$$\underline{\hspace{3cm}} \div \underline{\hspace{3cm}} = \underline{\hspace{3cm}}$$
Difference   Resting pulse   % Increase

I have found that my clients show a 20% to 30% increase in pulse rate after smoking. Heavy smokers actually show a decrease in heartrate at first. These nicotine-induced changes put a big strain on the heart. In fact, cigarette smoking is a factor in 120,000 U.S. deaths from coronary heart disease. By quitting smoking, you've reduced your chances of being another one of those statistics.

ALTERNATIVE COUNTER-CONDITIONING EXERCISE

Light up, inhale and cough up the smoke after each inhalation for the next 10 puffs. Inhale at your normal smoker's pace, as you repeat to yourself, or Buddy reads, the following messages:

10) Inhale and cough it up. "Smoking irritates my throat."

9) Inhale and cough it up. "Smoking irritates my eyes."

8) Inhale and cough it up. "Smoking leaves me with a bitter taste in my mouth."

7) Inhale and cough it up. "Smoking burns my lips and tongue."

6) Inhale and cough it up. "Smoking coats my lungs, teeth and body with tar."

5) Inhale and cough it up. "Smoking leaves me short of breath."

4) Inhale and cough it up. "Smoking leaves my throat feeling dry and scratchy."

3) Inhale and cough it up. "Smoking leaves my chest feeling heavy and congested."

2) Inhale cough it up. "Smoking leaves my chest feeling tight and congested, and I can't breathe."

1) Inhale and cough it up *hard*. "Cigarettes are beginning to lose some of their power over me. It's perfectly OK with me to put them out for the next 24 hours."

IF YOU STILL HAVE THE URGE TO SMOKE, REPEAT THIS LAST PORTION OF THE EXERCISE. DO NOT REPEAT IT MORE THAN ONCE.

Good. Put your cigarette out, discard the smoked butts in the glass jar, break the remaining cigarettes in half, and flush them down the toilet. Brush your teeth, drink some water, and join me back here when you're done.

VISUAL IMAGERY EXERCISE

Let's take a break from smoking and relax. I'd like you to close your eyes and take a deep breath in through your nose, and out through your mouth. Do this three times.

For the next few breaths, I'd like you to inhale slowly through the mouth and imagine that you are breathing all the way up to the top of your head, and exhaling the air down your body, down your legs, and out the souls of your feet into the ground.

Ready?

Inhale through your mouth, to the top of your head, down through your body, and out into the ground. Pretend that you are breathing all the static tension out of you, sending it down into the ground.

As you breathe in, feel the waves of the ocean circulating through your body. Every breath that you take is like a wave, cleansing and soothing.

Every breath fills you with energy, vigor and health. Feel your body grow stronger, as you feel the power over your habit grow stronger.

As the waves wash through your body, watch them wash away your former positive associations with smoking as you say to yourself:

- Cigarettes are no longer relaxing.
- They are no longer important in my life.
- I'm no longer willing to fill my body with dirt and poisons.

As you take another deep breath, notice how the symptoms you experienced during today's smoking session have almost completely faded.

When you close your eyes tonight to sleep, think back on the ocean cleaning your mind and body, breaking down the power smoking has over you.

When you have an urge to smoke today, concentrate on the negative, nauseous effects you experienced in today's session.

Continue to work with your breathing. Don't forget to take your vitamins. Also, review the *Quitter's Survival Guide,* page 148, and the *Deep Relaxation Exercise* on page 142.

IF YOU'RE PREGNANT, OR LIVE WITH CHILDREN PLEASE READ THIS!

More and more studies show that smoking during pregnancy has a significantly adverse effect upon the well-being of the fetus, the health of the newborn baby, and the future development of the infant and child.

According to the American Cancer Society's pamphlet, *Dangers Of Smoking/Benefits Of Quitting:*

● Women who smoke during pregnancy have significantly more stillbirths, and more of their babies die during the first month of infancy than those of non-smoking mothers.

● 20% of unsuccessful pregnancies would have been successful if the mother had not been a regular smoker.

● Babies of smoking mothers weigh about six ounces less than those of non-smoking mothers. The more a woman smokes during pregnancy, the less her infant will weigh. However, if a woman gives up smoking during pregnancy, her risk of delivering a low birth-weight baby becomes similar to that of a nonsmoker.

● When a pregnant woman smokes, the amount of carbon monoxide in the blood increases, depleting her fetus of oxygen.

● Dr. Elaine Confer, Attending Physician at Cedars Sinai Medical Center, and Clinical Instructor in Pediatrics at UCLA, has found that children of parents who smoke have more upper-respiratory infections and ear infections than patients of non-smoking parents.

Long-term follow-up studies show that children of mothers who smoked heavily during pregnancy are shorter in stature, have retarded reading ability and lower ratings on "social adjustment" than the children of non-smoking mothers.

TOMORROW'S SUPPLIES

For tomorrow's session, you will need one pack of your least favorite brand of cigarettes, a large glass jar filled with about two inches of water, a lighter or matches and mirror to watch yourself smoke—a shaving mirror is good.

DO NOT BUY YOUR CIGARETTES UNTIL RIGHT BEFORE YOUR SESSION. DO NOT OPEN THEM UNTIL YOU'RE INSTRUCTED TO DO SO, OR YOU WILL READDICT YOURSELF.

You're well on your way to "turning off" to smoking and breaking the positive associations you've developed with your smoking habit. Let me remind you again:

ONE PUFF ON A CIGARETTE—OTHER THAN THE SMOKING YOU ARE INSTRUCTED TO DO DURING THE PROGRAM—HAS THE POWER TO READDICT YOU!

Take the next few minutes to sign a contract with yourself to stop smoking for the next 24 hours. It's on the next page.

24-HOUR CONTRACT
TO QUIT SMOKING

I, _____ commit
to quitting smoking for the next 24 hours.

I've rid my environment of cigarettes, and will
not purchase any until directly before my next
session. I will not open this purchased pack until
instructed to do so.

I will use the techniques I've learned in this last
session to cope with the next 24 smokeless hours.

I am quitting smoking for myself, and of my own
free will and I'm choosing to do so for the following
reasons:

**LOOK THROUGH YOUR 3X5 CARDS.
FIND AND LIST HERE THE FIVE MOST
IMPORTANT BENEFITS YOU EXPECT TO
ATTAIN FROM QUITTING SMOKING, AND
THE FIVE MOST IMPORTANT
CONSEQUENCES YOU'VE INCURRED AS
A SMOKER.**

Benefits of Quitting

_____

_____

_____

_____

_____

Consequences of Smoking

_____

_____

_____

_____

_____

Signed _____

Date _____

Congratulations, ex-smoker. See you tomorrow at the same time.

Day 3: Why One Puff Readdicts

You've certainly heard it enough times, and you've seen enough examples from either your own past attempts at quitting or someone else's experience with relapse. *One puff readdicts.*

You may be wondering why, if one puff readdicts, I have you smoke during our sessions, and why those cigarettes don't re-hook you to smoking. The answer is that one puff readdicts you *psychologically*, not chemically. To readdict yourself back onto nicotine, you would need to smoke more than what you smoke during our sessions. Let me illustrate with an example from animal research.

THE RAT RACE

One of the most influential figures in modern psychology is B. F. Skinner, and one of his early contributions to behavioral psychology was the Skinner Box—a special box to study animal learning. When a rat is placed in it and pushes a lever, a mechanism delivers a pellet of food to the animal. The Skinner Box makes it possible to study different reward systems and their influence on animal behavior.

Let's imagine that a rat has been taught to press a food lever to obtain food. Each time the rat presses the lever, a food pellet falls out. This is called *continuous reinforcement*. In other words, 100% of all the rat's lever pressing leads to a reward—the food.

Let's say that this rat has been busily pressing away and eating for six months. One day, the experimenter shuts off the food reward "Cold Turkey." Now assuming that the rat is fed outside the cage so that it doesn't starve to death, how long will it take the rat to get the message that the food lever doesn't work any longer? In other words, how long does it take for this rat to "break" the bar-pressing habit? Well, it actually doesn't take very long at all. Within 2 to 3 days the rat is totally ignoring this food lever and has given up trying to obtain food from it.

Let's look at another situation. What would happen to this rat's bar-pressing habit if just before he was going to give up trying to obtain food by bar-pressing, a food pellet fell out? He would not only regain hope in the system, he would press the lever harder and more frequently than ever! This is called *intermittent reinforcement*. One food pellet would put this rat back into the habit of bar-pressing!

THE HUMAN RACE

Now let's plug *you* into this. As a smoker, just about every time you wanted a cigarette, you got it. Your urges to smoke were reinforced 100% of the time. When you started the program you were asked to stop smoking "Cold turkey." The only smoking you were permitted was the "turn off" smoking, which was neither rewarding, nor psychologically reinforcing. That's why it didn't readdict you. And by quitting "Cold Turkey," your urges to smoke will extinguish or fade over time— just as the rat's bar-pressing habit was broken when the behavior was no longer reinforced. Any habit that isn't rewarded or reinforced, in this case with a cigarette, fades over time.

But what would happen if you gave in to "just one puff" on a cigarette? I think you already know the answer: You would "re-ignite" your smoking habit. The 10% of the smoking habit you enjoyed would be intermittently reinforced. None of the other 90% negative associations would be remembered. You would experience amnesia as to why you stopped smoking. It's like giving an alcoholic a sip of liquor.

Once an addict, always an addict. Once addicted to tobacco, you can't retrain yourself to be a part-time smoker. If you think you can you're dreaming, or worse—lying to yourself. It's an all or nothing commitment, because one puff has the power to reinforce all the urges that made you give in and take that puff.

Here's why: If you say, "NO" a thousand times to smoking, and then finally give in with a YES, you reinforce those thousand urges with that one puff on a cigarette. Not only do you readdict yourself, but you strengthen your habit too. That one puff will start you smoking the same amount you smoked before you quit. One puff equals one pack, or two packs, five packs, or whatever was your usual daily need.

There's one last point I want to make before you open your pack of cigarettes: The obvious difference between you and the rat in the above example is that the rat has no real choice. As humans, we have choices, and it will always boil down to choosing—to smoke or not to smoke.

If you want to have an easy time as an ex-smoker, you do it by choosing to create a *no hope* situation for yourself. That's right. Don't give yourself *any hope* of smoking after today's session. That also means to not flirt with your urge to smoke. If you have an urge, nip it in the bud immediately. Do not build up a desire for a cigarette. Don't let it escalate.

When you adopt a no-hope, or no-chance-for-a-cigarette attitude, you are saying that you have predetermined the issue of whether or not you smoke and it is not up for discussion. Hope is the breeding ground for urges. Give up hope for a cigarette, and your urges to smoke will disappear.

Chemically, it takes about 72 hours for your body to rid itself of nicotine. Psychologically, it takes 21 days to change a habit. So stick with it. As time goes by you will find it easier and easier to not smoke.

Today is your last day of smoking. By tomorrow 72 hours will have passed and you will be out of withdrawal. But please remember that each individual's reaction time differs. So if you are still experiencing withdrawal symptoms, give it a little more time. You'll come out of it very soon.

Ready for a cigarette? I wouldn't be surprised if you're still anxious to smoke. Of course you are. You're still chemically addicted. You still need your "fix."

COUNTER-CONDITIONING SESSION

READ THE FOLLOWING EXERCISE BEFORE DOING IT.

Buddies, take turns coaching each other through this exercise.

You will need a shaving mirror or any good-sized mirror for this exercise because today you will *watch* yourself smoke.

To warm up, light your cigarette, inhale, and cough up the smoke. Do this three times.

From this point on you will be *puffing* without inhaling on two cigarettes at a time. Watch yourself in the mirror as you puff away at your favorite pacifier. Keep puffing until you're done with these two cigarettes, then light up two more and continue to puff on them, until they're finished.

Now stop and look at yourself in the mirror. Look familiar? Remember the last time you were at a party full of smokers and you chain-smoked through the drinks? Or remember when you stayed up late to finish a project and smoked until your eyes burned and teared?

Notice the taste in your mouth. How about the smell of smoke in your hair and on your clothes— smell familiar?

Now take out an unlit cigarette and, without lighting up, go through the motions of inhaling and exhaling as you watch yourself in the mirror. Notice your eyebrows furrowing together as you suck on the cigarette. Notice the tiny crow's feet lines around your eyes. Notice the fine lines around your mouth that your habit has etched into your face.

Notice your facial expression as you go through the motions of smoking. What does the body language of smoking convey to your children, your lover, your co-workers, to you? Think about this as you go through the motions of smoking.

Smokers assume awkward positions when they hold a cigarette. They either lean away from the smoke or hold their arm away so the smoke doesn't bother others or so it's near a window. Do you hunch over? Do you curl up? How does smoking effect your posture?

You've spent three sessions building negative associations with smoking. In your Sense Memory you have stored many negative sensations from your past smoking sessions.

Today, take a closer look at some of the visual "turn offs" of this habit. You can no longer hide behind the belief that smoking is attractive and sexy or relaxing and refreshing, or a harmless habit that only affects "the other guy."

There is no more purpose to smoking beyond this session. It's time to say goodbye to smoking once and for all.

GET OUT YOUR LAST CIGARETTE, AND LIGHT UP. YOU WILL BE INHALING AND COUGHING UP YOUR 10 LAST PUFFS OF A CIGARETTE AS YOU OR YOUR BUDDY REPEAT THE STATEMENTS BELOW:

10) Inhale and cough. "Smoking makes my lips burn."

9) Inhale and cough. "Smoking irritates my eyes."

8) Inhale and cough. "Smoking irritates my throat and makes it feel scratchy and uncomfortable."

7) Inhale and cough. "Smoking makes my chest feel heavy and congested."

6) Inhale and cough. "Smoking irritates my nose and causes my nose to feel dry and itchy."

5) Inhale and cough. "Smoking makes my stomach queasy."

4) Inhale and cough. "Smoking makes my head feel tight."

3) Inhale and cough. "Smoking puts my nerves on edge."

2) Inhale and cough. "Smoking makes me cough."

1) Inhale and cough it up for the last time. "Smoking makes me feel sick and dirty and I won't allow this habit to control me any longer. Goodbye cigarettes. I'm glad to be done with this habit once and for all!"

Congratulations! You'll never have to abuse your body with cigarettes again. Take the smoked butts, discard them in your jar, and break the rest of the cigarettes in half, and flush them down the toilet. Brush your teeth, drink some water, and join me back here when you're done.

HOW QUITTERS RELAPSE

I talked about why one puff puts you back on the hook again. Now I want to give you some examples of how quitters readdict themselves to cigarettes.
The Drinker—He tends to forget his commitments easily under the influence of alcohol. Pretty soon he's saying to himself "Aw, what the heck, one little puff can't really hurt."

When you drink, even the strongest resolve goes up in smoke. Don't fall into the trap of readdicting yourself over a glass of booze. If you're going to drink alcohol, drink only in the company of non-smokers. But better yet, play it safe and avoid alcohol for one month after quitting. Why take chances with your success?

The Curious Taster—She fools herself into believing that she's not really smoking. She goes around lighting others' cigarettes, claiming "I don't smoke anymore. I just enjoy the act of lighting up my friend's cigarettes for them." The Curious Taster is also the sort of person who thinks it's cute to show off how much control she has over smoking. Unfortunately, just one puff on a cigarette will readdict her.

The only safe cigarette is the unsmoked cigarette. The only way to control this addiction is to stay clear of trouble. Don't be a wise guy at your own expense. Save the tasting for the smokers. You are an *ex-smoker*, remember?

The Program Tester—He reminds me of The Curious Taster, but he's much more psychologically aware. He thinks he's got the program all figured out and wants to test out whether he's still "turned off" to smoking. He's out to prove the program wrong, and show himself that he can outsmart the system. And he's usually very successful at outsmarting himself right back into smoking again.

The counter-conditioning exercises were designed to turn you off to smoking. You don't need to be very psychologically sophisticated to know that if you smoke a cigarette, you are looking to enjoy it, not to turn yourself off to it.

If you want to know whether you will always be turned off to smoking, the answer is *not if you have a puff on it*. You will only stay turned off to smoking if you reinforce the negative sensations you experienced in your counter-conditioning sessions. Don't let your addict sabotage you into smoking again.

Special Occasion Smoker—She feels cheated out of her favorite reward in life—cigarettes. She's the type who wants her cake and eat it too. She wants to smoke only on special occasions, yet she wants to remain an ex-smoker.

She saves those special puffs for special moments, like after a romantic meal, or to celebrate a special event. It's her special reward, her special gift to herself.

The problem with this smoker is that after she takes that one special occasion puff, she gets to gift wrap her present at the tune of however many packs a day she smoked before!

Remember, one puff fully readdicts you to smoking the same amount you smoked before. You can't be a little bit of a smoker any more than you can be a little bit pregnant. It's black or white. Either you smoke, or you don't.

Forewarned is Forearmed—Save these special occasions to celebrate your continuing success as a strong and healthy ex-smoker.

I would rather you laugh at these characters now, than have you experience a relapse with smoking. The more aware you are of these potential traps for failure, the stronger a position you'll be in to say NO to smoking for good.

You're almost there. You'll probably be out of withdrawal by tomorrow. Don't forget to take your vitamins, and read through the *Quitter's Survival Guide* and *Deep Relaxation Exercise*.

PLEASE DON'T BRING ANY CIGARETTES TO TOMORROW'S SESSION. SAVE THE GLASS JAR AND BUTTS AS REMINDERS OF THE NASTY TASTE AND SMELL OF YOUR EX-SMOKING HABIT.

See you tomorrow.

CONTRACT TO QUIT SMOKING PERMANENTLY

I, _____ commit to quitting smoking permanently. I will continue to make 24-hour commitments to quit smoking for good—I know that this is a one-day-at-a-time process.

I've rid my environment of cigarettes, and will not purchase any more.

I will use the techniques I've learned in these last sessions to cope with the next 24 hours without a cigarette.

I am quitting smoking for myself, of my own free will and I'm choosing to do so for the following reasons:

LOOK THROUGH YOUR 3X5 CARDS. WRITE DOWN THE FIVE MOST IMPORTANT BENEFITS YOU EXPECT TO ATTAIN FROM QUITTING SMOKING, AND THE FIVE WORST CONSEQUENCES YOU'VE INCURRED AS A SMOKER.

Benefits of Quitting

_____
_____
_____
_____
_____

Consequences of Smoking

_____
_____
_____
_____
_____

Signed _____

Date _____

Day 4: Mourning The Loss Of Your Best Friend

If the dizziness, the spaciness, the inability to concentrate and the constant craving for tobacco are beginning to fade, it's because the nicotine has left your bloodstream and you're no longer chemically addicted. If you're still experiencing the symptoms of nicotine withdrawal, relax. Your body is just taking a little longer to rid itself of the drug.

But just because you may be through with withdrawal doesn't necessarily mean that you're home free yet. After all the time you've spent as a smoker, did you really expect your urges to disappear in a few short easy lessons? Let's be realistic. Adapting psychologically to not smoking is a step-by-step process. Each day gets easier and easier, but of course you may still miss cigarettes.

This is what I want to talk to you about today. If there's a feeling that something's missing in your life; if there's a feeling of emptiness; a feeling that you're at a loss for something to do or say; it's because not smoking leaves you with a gap. Until you adjust to your new non-smoking routine, that feeling will persist until it eventually fades.

There are some things you can do to ease the emptiness with which not smoking leaves you. Fill in that gap with an oral or tactile substitute. Fill in the gap with keeping busy. Fill it in with more constructive, creative ways of using your time. Fill it in with the pride of accomplishment—you broke this destructive habit.

In the meantime, be glad that your purse and pockets aren't cluttered up with cigarettes, lighters, matches and other smoking paraphernalia. Ladies, I bet you never knew your purse was nothing more than a giant cigarette case.

A SENSE OF LOSS

Sometimes this feeling of loss goes much deeper. Some quitters go through an intense and emotionally difficult time. Some actually go through a mourning process not unlike that of losing a best friend. After all, cigarettes were always there for you, always there to take away the pain, to keep you company during lonely nights, always there when you needed something to lean on.

Dr. Elizabeth Kubler-Ross, who researches death and the dying, found that those who are about to lose, or have lost a loved one go through certain stages of mourning. I have found that some quitters go through a similar experience.

When a smoker quits smoking, there first is anger and denial of the loss. Then there is bargaining with themselves followed by feelings of sadness and depression, and finally acceptance of the loss. Hope is the one thing that persists until the quitter reaches acceptance.

Anger—If you're feeling angry, it's just that rebellious kid inside of you kicking up a last fight and yelling "I don't want to be uncomfortable! Give me back my pacifier." Even the most mature individuals find themselves regressing to this childlike state.

Be understanding and empathetic to this "kid" in you. Talk back. You might say "I know I'm angry, but I get even angrier thinking about how cigarettes controlled me for so many years. Besides, I'd rather be a temporarily angry person, than a permanently sick person."

Denial and Bargaining—Denial and bargaining often go hand in hand. You may think "I can quit for 24 hours at a time. I'll even quit for another 24 hours if you promise that you'll let me smoke tomorrow."

You may be getting through smoking one day at a time by fooling yourself that quitting is a temporary situation. Sometimes this is necessary to get through the short term. You were able to keep your word to quitting for 24 hours because we made a bargain that you could smoke during our sessions.

But at some point you deniers and bargainers have to face reality and resolve to a lifetime commitment. Now this doesn't mean that you should no longer quit smoking 24 hours at a time. You can still face the reality of quitting permanently while making day-by-day time commitments. All big changes start with a continuous series of small, manageable steps.

Sadness—If you feel sad, it's because you are saying goodbye to something you looked at as a companion. Even if that companion was doing you harm, it's one you've known intimately for a long time.

The point is this: You may feel sad; you may feel angry; you may feel depressed and lost. Notice your feelings. Realize that they are perfectly natural. And then go on leading your life.

So cry and rage if you want to. You'll find that after the sadness, comes acceptance, and eventually relief—knowing that you are no longer under the spell of smoking.

IF YOU STILL HAVE VERY STRONG URGES TO SMOKE, GO BACK TO YESTERDAY'S EXERCISE AND USE YOUR SENSE MEMORY TO RECREATE THE FEELINGS YOU EXPERIENCED DURING THE COUNTER-CONDITIONING SESSION.

DO NOT SMOKE THROUGH THESE EXERCISES. YOU DON'T WANT TO PUT ANY MORE NICOTINE INTO YOUR BLOODSTREAM BECAUSE YOU'RE ALMOST OUT OF WITHDRAWAL.

Congratulations, ex-smoker. As always, take quitting one day at a time. Continue to take your vitamins, review the *Quitter's Survival Guide* and use the *Deep Relaxation Exercise* to help relieve stress buildup. See you tomorrow.

Day 5: Creating A Positive Non-Smoking Image

Years ago, when you bought your first pack of cigarettes, you made a contract with the tobacco company. Without realizing it, you agreed to buy their product no matter what the cost. And you continued to use this product in spite of its bad taste, bad smell and bad affects on your body. Some of you chose it over your friends or your spouses. Many of you even chose heart disease, emphysema and cancer over not smoking. In short, you continued to honor your contract with the tobacco company no matter what the consequence were.

'TIL DEATH DO US PART

How did the tobacco companies seduce more than 50 million Americans? There are two answers: The first is addiction . . . the cigarette's magical quality that makes it a marketer's dream. What could be a more perfect product to sell than one with a little something to make the buyer want more and more all the time?

The second aspect to your 'til-death-do-us-part contract with the tobacco company is image. It's probably why you began smoking in the first place. Image is why you endured the dizziness and the nausea of your first few cigarettes. Image is probably why you chose your brand.

To create an image that captivates you into making your contract with your brand, tobacco companies spend millions of dollars a year in marketing, advertising and package design. You know the images I'm talking about: The strongly independent, self-reliant cowboy. The successful and sexy liberated woman. Cool, refreshing, or aggressive modern sexuality. Urban sophistication. The tobacco companies have worked hard to create them. And they've been extremely successful. After all, they hooked *you*, didn't they?

Well congratulations; you unhooked yourself. But because of all those years and millions of dollars, the tobacco companies have conditioned you to view smoking in a positive way. You now have to put a little effort into reconditioning yourself out of this image. Ex-smoker, it's time to shed your old smoking image.

RECONDITIONING EXERCISE

Sit back comfortably in a chair and imagine that

you are smoking your ideal cigarette. Allow your-self to flirt with it. Feel the satisfaction from each inhalation, the sense of comfort, security and familiarity. See the sophisticated *you* as you partake of this special pleasure.

I want you to switch scenes. You are now in a beautiful spot. The air is fresh and clean; the sky is very blue; and you feel fresh, clean, strong, relaxed and confident. Your body is like a finely tuned instrument in perfect balance with the environment. You can feel your heart beating steadily, rhythmically, like the waves. Your breathing is easy, deep and satisfying. Taste the clean fresh feeling in your mouth. Smell the fresh scent of your body. See the strong, glowing, non-smoking *you!*

Now I'd like you to go back to your fabulous cigarette. This time the cigarette tastes just a little too bitter, a little too hot. The sense of familiarity, comfort, and security is clouded over with a smokey, bitter and congested feeling. You want to cough.

Now go back to your soothing scene. Practice switching back and forth between the two images until the image of you as a smoker starts losing it's familiarity. Watch the positive image of being an ex-smoker grow stronger as your feelings about smoking start taking on more negative overtones.

And if you want to have a little fun, picture yourself as the rugged cowboy, out in the fields with your horse—a cigarette in one hand and an oxygen mask in the other. Or picture yourself as the sexy and sophisticated smoker—with yellow, tar-stained teeth, bad breath, and a smoker's cough. The next time you see a smoking advertisement, use your imagination to rip the false messages to shreds.

Congratulations, ex-smoker! You've kicked the habit! The only thing left to do is to *stay quit permanently*.

Staying Quit

In this chapter you'll find five sections that will help you *stay quit permanently!* Reread and use them whenever you have the urge to smoke or use food as a substitute.

HABIT BREAKERS HOT LINE

In 1978, UCLA established a crisis-intervention Stay-Quit hot line. It was a seven-day-a-week service for quitters. The hot line was set up to stop cigarette quitters from relapsing. Before the smoker would light up a cigarette, he or she would call to get help from a trained counselor ready to assist. In

November 1980, this federally-funded hot line ran out of money, but the project sparked an idea that proved a valuable tool for the Habit Breakers program.

When I opened Habit Breakers, I incorporated a 24-hour hot line into the program. Before enrolling in the Habit Breakers program, each client must agree that instead of lighting up a cigarette, he or she had to call the hot-line for crisis-intervention counseling first.

From my experience handling calls with hundreds of quitters, I learned valuable information: Why smokers relapse, and how best to counsel them through their urge to smoke.

I'd like to share some of the typical conversations I've had with my clients in the hopes that you can learn how to counsel yourself out of a relapse.

THE UPSET WOMAN

One client called me months after quitting smoking. She was very agitated when she related the following incident:

Ex-smoker—My car was robbed. I had just bought it the other day, and now it's gone. I'm so angry I could explode. I need to calm down. I need a cigarette.

Judy—You really sound upset. It would have been so easy for you to go to a store and get a pack of cigarettes rather than place this call, but you didn't. I know that you'd like to smoke, but you really don't want to go back to smoking.

Ex-smoker—That's true. But I'd sure like to have a cigarette this minute.

Judy—It sounds like you just want to dump this anger inside of you and then get on with life as an ex-smoker.

Ex-smoker—Yes.

Judy—Amy, you've been off cigarettes for 3 months now. You've successfully handled many stressful events in this time frame. What has kept you from smoking?

Ex-smoker—Knowing that lighting up won't make the situation better. I've been through too much while kicking this habit to start smoking again.

Judy—OK, I want to remind you that deep breathing helps calm you down when you're anxious. How about taking a few deep breaths now . . . breathing in through your nose, all the way up to the top of your head, and down your body, into the ground, letting all that stress out. Feel how clear and uncongested your chest feels. Reaffirm your decision to remain quit. Do you remember why you chose to kick the habit?

Ex-smoker—Yes. I want to be able to exercise better, and I want to be in control of my life and not have cigarettes control me.

Judy—Sounds to me like you're ready to get on with things and deal with this unfortunate incidence without smoking. Can I get a commitment that you won't smoke for the next 24 hours?

Ex-smoker—Yes, absolutely.

Judy—Let's talk again tomorrow.

THE EXPLOSIVE EMPLOYEE

Ex-smoker—I can't stand working for my boss any longer. I want to tell him what I really think of him, then flatten his face against the wall.

Judy—And you're really angry because on top of that you can't even numb these feelings by sucking them down with a cigarette.

Ex-smoker—Sure. It's not easy to resist reaching for a cigarette when I'm feeling this way. Sometimes I want to say "What the heck. Life's hard enough without trying to quit smoking too." I'm calling because I made a commitment to call you before lighting up a cigarette, and I want you to know that I have one in my hand now.

Judy—OK John. How is smoking going to make your life better?

Ex-smoker—Well, for one, it will keep me from saying or doing something I may regret later.

Judy—It sounds as though you think you'll really hurt someone—or worse, hurt yourself by saying the wrong thing and getting fired for it.

Ex-smoker—That's right.

Judy—What's the worst thing that can happen from feeling this way?

Ex-smoker—I told you, I can lose control, punch the guy out, or say the wrong thing and get fired.

Judy—But you didn't, did you? You left the situation to make this phone call, didn't you?

Ex-smoker—That's true.

Judy—So John, what's the worse thing that can happen when you feel this angry?

Ex-smoker—I suppose I can just leave . . .

Judy—Sure. If it gets too uncomfortable, leave the situation, cool off, and when you feel better, go back and work things out. I'd like to go through the Sense Memory exercise with you before we hang up the phone.

Ex-smoker—Sure.

Judy—I want you to imagine that you just lit the cigarette in your hand. Picture yourself inhaling the heavy, sooty, bitter smoke. Feel your chest swell with congestion. Can you feel that?

Ex-smoker—Yes.

Judy—Now use your Sense Memory to bring back the dizziness, the irritability, and the nausea that you experienced in the course of your treatment.

Ex-smoker—OK, I've got it.

Judy—Now I want you to cough *hard*. Again, *harder*. Is it OK with you not to smoke for the next 24 hours?

Ex-smoker—Yes, I'm fine.

Judy—Then what do you say to ripping up that cigarette in your hand?

Ex-smoker—Fine.

Judy—Let's talk tomorrow. By the way, I think it took a lot of integrity for you to call before readdicting yourself. You'll make it through because you're someone who keeps his word. Call me again if you need to.

THE CAGED ANIMAL

Ex-smoker—I feel like a caged animal. I keep pacing back and forth and I don't know how to calm down.

Judy—For eight years you've been calming yourself down with a cigarette. It's no wonder you feel this way.

Ex-smoker—And smoking helped me take my mind off of whatever was bothering me too.

Judy—It has been only 48 hours since you quit smoking. You're experiencing the anxiety of nicotine withdrawal. When you're going through withdrawal, it's easy to forget the fact that you *chose* to quit smoking. Sometimes it starts to look like quitting smoking was imposed by an outside force rather than chosen by you. Remember, you're not a caged animal, you're freer than you ever were because *you,* and not your *cigarettes* are calling the shots on your smoking habit. It's tough to go through what you're experiencing, yet if you hang in there just a little while longer, you'll be past this point and feeling differently about things. In the mean time, let's go through a deep breathing exercise to help you relax. Starting with a deep breath in through the nose, breathe all the way up to the top of your head, and exhale the stress of the day down your body, into the ground. Do that a couple of times until you feel more grounded and less anxious. Can I get a commitment from you to hang in there another 24 hours and not smoke?

Ex-smoker—I'm not sure.

Judy—Can I get a commitment for 12 hours?
Ex-smoker—Yes, because I'm going to bed soon and I can't smoke in my sleep, fortunately.
Judy—I'll call you in the morning and see how you feel.

HOT LINE IN THE MAILS

Instead of a hot-line call, I once got a hot-line postcard from a young law student and client of mine. He was vacationing in France and must have had a hard time because he wrote me the following:

Dear Judy,
I'm having a great time . . . well, that's not the whole truth. It's easier to forget your commitment when you're out of town. I had to write you and let you know that it's tough not smoking, but I'm recommitting to not smoking.

THE OBSESSIVE
FORMER SMOKER

Ex-smoker—I'm starting to obsess about smoking again. I can't get cigarettes out of my mind. It's just a matter of time before I give into this nagging urge.
Judy—You feel like a walking time bomb ready to explode with cigarettes.
Ex-smoker—Right. I just want to get cigarettes off my mind, and the only way to stop obsessing about them is by giving in to them.
Judy—You lost another job, didn't you? And you want to smoke to numb the pain?

Ex-smoker—How did you guess?

Judy—What are you doing about getting another job?

Ex-smoker—Obsessing about cigarettes.

Judy—I see. Smoking makes you passive. It prevents you from taking action, and it also prevents you from failing too many times. It's like a safety valve. Obsess about smoking, and you don't have to face your pain, anger and disappointment. Sheila, you already made the decision to quit smoking. The decision to smoke or not to smoke is not up for discussion. There's clearly only one thing left to do.

Ex-smoker—What's that?

Judy—Keep your word to yourself! Do you want to see your urges disappear?

Ex-smoker—Yes.

Judy—Then put yourself on the line 100%. Can you commit to quitting smoking for 24 hours?

Ex-smoker—I guess so . . .

Judy—Well guessing isn't good enough. You have to put yourself on the line 100%.

Ex-smoker—I feel like it's a no-win situation. When I smoke, I want to quit. When I'm not smoking, I want to light up. Is there any hope for me?

Judy—No. Hoping to succeed doesn't work either Sheila. Put yourself on the line with this. Give me a definite commitment to quit smoking for the next 24 hours.

Ex-smoker—OK. You have a commitment for 24 hours.

Judy—Now watch your urge to smoke disappear. Remember: Urges feed on hope. If there's no hope for a cigarette, urges are of no value in your life. Enjoy an unobsessive day. I'll talk to you tomorrow.

WEIGHT CONTROL

Quitting smoking and gaining weight don't necessarily have to go together. Even though gaining weight is a big concern for most quitters, only one third of those who quit smoking gain weight. And they do so because they end up substituting food for cigarettes. They tend to "abuse" food as they "abused" cigarettes.

It makes perfect sense. You can suck your feelings down with a cigarette, and you can swallow them down with food. You can pacify yourself with cigarettes, and you can pacify yourself with food. You can reduce stress by smoking, and you can do it with food. You can pick your energy up with a cigarette, and you can do it with a candy bar too. You can see why it would be easy to make the switch from one habit to another.

Starting today, you're going to apply some of the same techniques you learned to handle your smoking urge, to the eating urge. Starting today, you're going to say NO to gaining excess weight and say NO to allowing it to sabotage your success with quitting smoking.

The obvious big difference between giving up smoking and giving up overeating is that you can "Cold Turkey" on cigarettes, but you can't "Cold Turkey" on food. Nor would you want to. But what you *can* do is stop the attitudes, behaviors, and bad food choices that create excess weight gain.

Let's take a look at what you can do to gain control of overeating.

RULE 1: DON'T DIET

If you want to lose weight and keep it off, you have to give up dieting. Dieting doesn't work, and it doesn't work because first, you can't stay on a diet for the rest of your life. Second, the mind is set up so that it remembers everything you wanted to eat when you were on a diet. And then, in an act of rebellion, it attacks everything you were so successful at avoiding during the diet.

The resultant effect is the *yo-yo syndrome*. You go on a diet. Your weight comes off. You feel deprived. You gain it all back again. Then you start the cycle all over again. I'm sure you know living examples of this pattern.

THE YO-YO SYNDROME

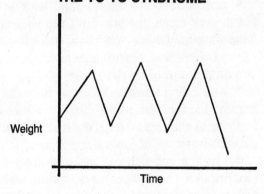

RULE 2: MAKE EVERY MEAL COUNT

What *does* work is the opposite of depriving yourself. You want to make every meal special. You want to make eating an orally and sensually satisfying experience. And you can do that without eating fattening foods and without gaining excess weight. It simply takes a little imagination and effort.

When you quit smoking,there's a tendency to adopt a "Poor me, I'm so deprived" attitude. The addict mind, with which you are well familiar, can start acting up by saying "If I can't smoke, I'm going to indulge myself in food instead." You *can* indulge yourself in food—the smart way.

● Why not make every meal count? Why not set your table with your best linen and china?

● Every dinner can be a dinner by candle light. Every meal can be special.

● And just because you're cutting back on alcohol doesn't mean that you can't use your crystal wine glasses. Didn't you know that club soda, mineral water and tomato juice taste better when you drink it out of crystal glasses?

● And eating salad doesn't have to be dull and boring. Explore the many different varieties of fresh herbs and vegetables at the supermarket. Try different varieties of low-calorie dressings.

● Chicken and fish can make exciting dishes too. Sprinkle your baked fish or chicken with dill, tarragon, or rosemary. Squeeze some fresh lemon or lime over it to give it a tangy flavor.

● And who needs to eliminate desserts? Have you checked out the many fruits in season? How do fresh strawberries, blueberries, or raspberries sound? Now that your sense of taste and smell is better than ever, you can enjoy the subtleties of good food.

RULE 3: EAT SLOWLY

When you sit down to a wonderful meal, make it a time to relax. Put on some soft music, take the phone off the hook, and enjoy your meal. Eating slowly is a key to losing weight. Take the time to slow down.

It takes 20 minutes for the brain to get the message that your stomach is full, so if you slow down your eating, you will feel full and satisfied after 20 minutes.

To help you slow down, put your fork and knife down between bites. Chew slowly, enjoying each and every morsel of food. And if you find yourself wolfing down a meal, take a deep breath and remind yourself that eating slowly will prevent you from overeating and gaining excess pounds.

RULE 4: USE ORAL SUBSTITUTES

And what about between meals? What about the need to satisfy your oral urge? Don't worry. Most of the time what you have in your mouth is not as important as having something to keep it busy with. Popcorn, rice cakes, celery, carrots, green peppers, sunflower seeds (watch the quantity because they are high in calories), sugarless gum or mints, a straw, a coffee stirrer or toothpick, or even a cinnamon stick can satisfy this oral need.

If you have the urge to eat, drink a glass of water or some herb tea before reaching for food. You may find that your urge will go away. Brush your teeth, or spray your mouth with mouthwash. You'll think twice about eating when your breath tastes sweet and clean. It's a good idea to get in the habit of brushing your teeth right after eating. Make it a ritual that ends each meal.

RULE 5: DON'T SKIP OR SKIMP ON MEALS

If you want to lose weight, you want to make sure that you are eating well. It may sound like a contradiction, but it's not.

If you skip or skimp on your meals, you'll feel hungry between meals and have a tendency to either snack or overeat when you finally do sit down to eat.

Eat three meals a day. Start with a high-protein breakfast, a good sized lunch, and a light, nutritious dinner. And if you must have a certain fattening dessert (don't deprive yourself of an occasional one), eat it after a meal. You may eat less of it this way.

RULE 6: CUT DOWN ON YOUR PORTIONS

Here are five easy ways to cut down on portions:
- Clean out your house of fattening foods. Out of sight is out of mind.

● Serve your portions from the stove. It will deter you from continuously spooning out extra portions.

● Don't eat everything on your plate. Make a point of leaving some leftovers.

● When dining out, order a la carte. You can always order more if you're still hungry. And ask the waiter to not bring bread and butter.

● Split a meal with a friend.

RULE 7: EAT ONLY AT THE DINING TABLE

Eat only at the table and don't mix it with other activities such as reading, or watching TV. You'd be surprised how easy it is to get carried away with the plot of a good book, or a TV program and get carried away with the portion you're eating at the same time.

RULE 8: "TURN ON" TO THIN FOODS. "TURN OFF" TO FAT FOODS

Just as you were able to use your Sense Memory to "turn off" to smoking, you can use it to "turn on" to low-calorie foods and "turn off" to fattening foods. Try this exercise now:

I want you to imagine that you have just eaten a fresh, light, nutritious salad. Taste the subtle flavors of the vegetables. Smell the fine aroma of fresh dill. Experience how satisfied and good you feel afterwards.

Now I want you to imagine that you just polished

off your favorite junk food. You feel stuffed, greasy, bloated and crampy. The food doesn't sit right with you because it was too heavy for your system.

I would like you to practice going back and forth between the image of eating a nutritiously satisfying meal, and overstuffing yourself on junk, until the first starts feeling more and more right to you.

It takes 21 days to form a new habit. Get in the practice of good eating habits. Within a short time, these habits will be ingrained.

Take these steps towards behavioral change one day at a time, 24 hours at a time and prove to yourself that you can quit smoking, and keep your weight under control too!

PREVENTING RELAPSE

Let's look at the eight most common traps for failure:

- Life crisis—death of a loved one, sickness or divorce
- Drinking alcohol and abusing drugs
- Eating with smokers
- Relaxing after dinner
- Pressure or frustration at work
- Arguments
- Depression
- Boredom

Chances are that readdiction would occur under one of these circumstances. As you read the two following scenarios, pretend that these situations are happening to you. Think about how you would behave under these circumstances.

DRINKING SCENARIO

It's after work. You were just promoted to a higher position and the gang decides to take you out for a drink to celebrate. It occurs to you that you shouldn't be drinking so soon after you quit smoking, but you figure "How often do I get promoted?" You order *just one* glass of wine to play it safe, of course. Certainly one glass of wine won't get you drunk.

You're starting to loosen up now . . . you're feeling great and order another round of drinks. The cigarette in the ashtray next to you is looking better and better the longer you stare at it. You just can't seem to unglue your eyes from it. Your fingers reach out to pick it out of the ashtray . . .

Take a few seconds to see this situation. See yourself reaching for the cigarette in the ashtray.

STOP! GET YOUR FINGERS AWAY FROM THAT CIGARETTE!

Now take a deep breath, and flood your senses with the negative sensations you've developed with your smoking habit in today's smoking session. Bring back that bitter, harsh taste, the feeling of nausea, the congestion and irritation in your chest. Cough, clear your throat, and *get out of there! Go home!* Or if you won't do that, at least go to the bathroom, splash some cold water on your face, brush your teeth, take a few deep breaths and come back sober.

Let's go over these coping skills again: You're just about to pick up a cigarette.

STOP! RECALL YOUR "TURN OFF" FEELINGS ABOUT SMOKING. WASH YOUR FACE, BRUSH YOUR TEETH, TAKE A DEEP BREATH AND LEAVE!

The more you practice this exercise, the more automatic your response to a similar situation will be. When you're drunk and vulnerable to smoking, you don't want to be figuring out what to do to prevent yourself from relapsing. You'll be much more effective at remaining quit if you have the scene worked out beforehand.

Now let me ask you this: What's wrong with the situation you just read about? The answer is obvious. You shouldn't have been out drinking with the gang so soon after quitting smoking! I *strongly* suggest that you stay away from alcohol and any other drugs that can interfere with your decision-making abilities for at least one month after quitting smoking. If you're going to drink alcohol, at least make sure that you're not around alcohol and cigarettes at the same time.

ARGUMENT SCENARIO

You've just had a major argument with your spouse or lover. The options look clear: You either attack the person, or a pack of cigarettes. Old memories about smoking and its many wonderful uses come back to you. Remember how it soothed your nerves when you were angry. How it helped you get along better with your relationships? How it helped you through those tense moments?

Before you say or do something that you may regret later, you run out of the house, shaking with anger. You drive down to the drugstore, and there, on top of the grocer's shelf is your relief. You're just about to rip open the package of cigarettes and eat them alive . . .

STOP! TEAR THAT PACKAGE TO SHREDS AND TRASH IT!

Or better yet, return it to the grocer, get your money plus tax back, and buy yourself a present. How about a magazine?

Let's go through this scene again, this time carefully thinking through what you could have done instead of going to the store to buy a pack of cigarettes. It's certainly easier to say NO to smoking before you have that pack between your addict's fingers.

What are some other options? How about cooling off emotionally before acting impulsively? Take a shower—you can't smoke in the shower anyway. Jogging is good—run off that tension. Punch a pillow if it will make you feel better. And when you've cooled down, take a direct approach to handling what's bothering you.

Now that you're not smoking, you need to get off your chest what you've been sucking down with a cigarette. Let your partner know how you feel without blaming, criticizing, judging, moralizing or yelling. Clear the air by communicating effectively. It's the best relief possible—even better than smoking. When you give yourself this relief, you may find that the urge to smoke disappears.

IN CASE OF RELAPSE

You will need one pack of your least favorite

brand of cigarettes, a lighter and matches, and a glass jar filled with about two inches of water.

IF YOU'VE BEEN SMOKING FOR LESS THAN 24 HOURS, READ THE FOLLOWING EXERCISE.

IF YOU'VE BEEN SMOKING FOR MORE THAN A DAY, YOU MAY HAVE TO REPEAT THE FIRST THREE DAYS OF THE PROGRAM TO SUCCESSFULLY QUIT SMOKING AGAIN.

BEFORE YOU REPEAT THEM, DO THE EXERCISES IN THIS SECTION.

If you feel guilty that you smoked or if you feel embarrassed that you've let yourself down, I want you to know that it takes a lot of integrity to keep your word to yourself and get back on track as an ex-smoker. The fact that you're reading this is evidence that you want to quit again. And you will. Starting *now!*

So let's leave guilt, shame, and feeling like a failure on the sidelines.

The good news is that if you've smoked only a few cigarettes, you aren't totally chemically readdicted. You get a break from having to go through nicotine withdrawal all over again. The bad news is that you did psychologically readdict yourself, and you've probably found out the hard way that one puff does indeed readdict you.

As a matter of fact, by smoking, you have wiped out all the negative associations you've worked so hard on establishing in your counter-conditioning sessions. So to help you re-establish those negative associations, you are going to do some more "turn off" smoking today.

But first, take a few minutes to again remember your five most important consequences and benefits of smoking:

Consequences From Smoking

_____

_____

_____

_____

_____

Benefits Of Quitting

_____

_____

_____

_____

_____

As you go through the following exercise, keep these reasons for quitting in the forefront of your mind.

Read the exercise first, before lighting up a cigarette. Ready? Take out a cigarette, and light it up.

10) Inhale. Suck it down deep into your chest, and cough it up. Hard.

9) Inhale and cough it up again.

8) Inhale, cough it up, and feel the bitter heat on your lips and tongue.

7) Inhale, cough it up, and feel the heat and congestion in your chest.

6) Inhale and cough it up. Remember the entire package deal of smoking—the coughing, the smell, the congestion, the lack of energy.

5) Inhale and cough it up again.

4) Inhale and cough it up and feel the irritation in your throat.

3) Inhale and cough it up and feel the irritation in your chest.

2) Inhale and cough it up as you say to yourself: "Smoking is not worth the trouble, the expense and the pain. My life will not only be OK without this habit, but it will be much better without it.

1) Inhale and cough it up for the last time, and say goodbye to your last cigarette.

REPEAT THIS EXERCISE UNTIL YOUR URGE TO SMOKE DISAPPEARS.

NOTE: DO NOT SMOKE MORE THAN TWO CIGARETTES THIS WAY. PLEASE STOP THE EXERCISE IF YOU FEEL SICK.

Put the cigarette butt out in the jar of water, break the remaining cigarettes in half and flush them down the toilet. Brush your teeth, drink some water, and join me back here when you're done.

RELAPSE ANALYSIS

Let's take a moment to study the situation that caused you to relapse:

How long were you off cigarettes since you relapsed? _____

How long have you been smoking since you last quit? _____

When did you take your first puff on a cigarette?

_____

How soon afterwards did you need another cigarette? _____

How much have you smoked since you readdicted yourself? _____

Where were you when you lit up? _____

Who were you with? _____

How were you feeling before you lit up? _____

How did you feel after you lit up? _____

How did the first puff of the relapse cigarette taste?

_____

What triggered your urge to smoke? _____

Why did you decide to quit again? _____

Take a few minutes to look over what you just wrote. What would you do differently today in that same situation?

_____

_____

_____

_____

_____

_____

_____

_____

_____

_____

_____

_____

_____

I can't overemphasize the importance of getting back on track immediately if you relapse. Once you're smoking, it's very difficult to break away from your habit and it's even harder to remember why you chose to quit in the first place.

TAKE A MOMENT TO SIGN A CONTRACT WITH YOURSELF AND RENEW YOUR COMMITMENT TO QUITTING SMOKING.

CONTRACT TO QUIT SMOKING

I, _____ am renewing my commitment to quit smoking starting NOW.

If I have urges to smoke, I will refer to the *Quitter's Survival Guide* to help me through each day.

Tonight I will take the time to do the *Deep Relaxation Exercise*.

If I relapse to smoking, I commit to getting back on track within 24 hours by reviewing the section called *Preventing Relapse*.

I commit to continuing to make 24-hour commitments to myself to quit smoking.

Signed _____

Date _____

Congratulations, ex-smoker. Your reasons for quitting are obviously too important to allow a relapse to get in your way. Good for you!

DEEP RELAXATION EXERCISE

This exercise is based on the Dunlap Relaxation Exercise. It's meant to be used daily to help you relieve stress, reaffirm your reasons for quitting smoking, and help you fall asleep.

As you're probably well aware, quitting smoking is both physically and emotionally draining, so take this time to allow your mind and body to completely relax. For this exercise, you will need five to ten minutes of quiet time.

PLEASE READ AND MAKE SURE YOU UNDERSTAND THE ENTIRE EXERCISE BEFORE YOU START.

Sit or lie down in a comfortable spot. Kick off your shoes, loosen any tight clothing, and make sure you won't be disturbed.

Start with a deep breath in through your nose and take this breath all the way up to the top of your head. Then as you exhale slowly, allow the breath to travel down your body, through your legs, and out the soles of your feet, down into the ground. If you feel uncomfortable breathing nasally, breathe through your mouth instead.

Allow any thoughts, worries, or tensions of the day to buzz through your head. Notice these thoughts and feelings and let them be there. Notice where you store stress in your body.

- Breathe in, hold it for five seconds, and feel

the tension drain out of you as you exhale down your body, and out the soles of your feet into the ground.

● As you take another breath in, you're going to squeeze your eyes shut as tightly as you can, hold it for five seconds. Let the tension go as you exhale down your body into the ground.

● Continue to inhale, tensing the muscle you're working on. Hold the tension for five seconds, then release and breathe down your body into the ground as you work on relaxing different muscle groups.

● If you get a cramp, stretch out the muscle slowly and rub it down.

● Breathe in. Tense the scalp muscles by raising your eyebrows as high as you can. Hold it for five seconds. Then exhale as you release.

● Breathe in. Tense the jaw muscles by biting down as hard as you can. Hold it. Then exhale as you let the tension go.

● Breathe in, tensing facial muscles by grimacing. Bigger. Hold it and let it go.

● Moving to the shoulders, inhale as you scrunch up your shoulders to your ears. Tighter. Hold it and exhale as you let go of the tension. Rotate your shoulders and release any tension there.

● Breathe in, and make a tight fist. Hold it and let it go as you exhale.

● Now for the biceps. Make a muscle as you breathe in. Hold it. Then let it go and shake it out as you exhale.

- Breathe in. Tense the entire arm. Hold it and exhale as you let it go and shake out your arm.

- Breathe in deeply, filling your lungs so you feel your back muscles and rib cage get a good stretch. Hold it for seven seconds and let go. Repeat.

- Moving to the stomach muscles, take a deep breath and tighten your stomach. Hold it and let it go as you breathe out.

- Breathe in, tightening your buttock muscles. Hold it and let go.

- Breathe in, tighten your thighs muscles. Exhale as you let go the tension.

- Breathe in, tightening your leg muscles. Make them as rigid as logs. Hold it. Tighter. Then release as you exhale.

- Check your body for tension points. Breathe in. Tighten the tense muscle and as you exhale, pretend that tension is draining out of you down into the ground.

- End the exercise with a deep breath to the top of your head, and exhale that breath down your body, breathing any remaining tension down into the ground.

- Notice that you were able to create a feeling of relaxation and tranquility without a cigarette.

CONTINUE TO BREATHE DEEPLY AND RELAX AS YOU ACKNOWLEDGE THE BENEFITS OF QUITTING SMOKING.

As you're sitting or lying down this very minute, your body is healing and cleansing. By quitting smoking today, you've made a tremendous difference to your well being.

Because you've quit smoking, you've already decreased your heart rate and blood pressure. Without the vasoconstricting action of nicotine restricting the bloodflow in your arteries, your heart doesn't have to pump as hard to bring a fresh supply of oxygenated blood to your brain, limbs, and organs. By quitting smoking, you've actually relieved your body of stress equivalent to that of 100 pounds of excess fat!

Take a deep breath and become aware of the strong steady rhythm of your heart. Feel the burden of stress lift as you visualize your blood flowing easily through open vessels. As you exhale, breathe out that burden of stress you've been carrying around as a smoker.

Because you're not smoking, you've made a tremendous difference in your body chemistry. As a smoker, you were constantly flooding your body with nicotine, jangling your nerves and throwing your energy off balance. The nicotine rush that gave you that temporary lift and the following nicotine depressant are no longer affecting your mood.

Take a deep breath and visualize your body chemistry finding a new equilibrium. Your nerves are steadier; your mood is calmer; and your energy level is higher. As you exhale, imagine that you are exhaling the poisonous chemicals from smoking.

Continue to breathe as you notice how uncongested your lungs feel, how much easier it is to take deeper, more satisfying breaths. In the next six months to a year, your lungs will be clear of most of the tar you've inhaled as a smoker. Within 7 to 10 years, provided you haven't done irreparable damage, your lungs will look like those of someone who's never smoked.

As your body continues to repair itself, you may find that you sleep better, that you have more energy throughout the day, and perhaps even think clearer. The oxygen increase makes it possible for the brain to function more efficiently. This extra oxygen also makes you look younger, brighter and more refreshed. Many ex-smokers look and feel years younger after quitting smoking.

The benefits of quitting are already a part of your experience as an ex-smoker. Isn't it great not smelling like a pack of cigarettes? And isn't it a relief not needing a nicotine fix every 20 minutes or so? Or running out in the middle of the night because you're out of the drug? Or worrying about social affairs and whether you can smoke at so-and-so's house? Or missing the end of a show because you need to leave the theatre to smoke? Or not being able to participate in physical activities because you get winded?

And isn't it a pleasure to walk into your house or apartment and have it smell fresh and clean instead of stale and dirty from smoke? And doesn't it feel good not burning up hundreds of dollars on a habit that, for the most part, you never enjoyed?

What a relief it is to finally stop fighting with yourself about quitting and having to quit.

You made a commitment to kick this habit and you'll stick to it because the payoffs for not smoking are incredible.

As you go through each day, keep looking for the benefits of quitting smoking. After all, if you're getting a payoff from remaining quit, you'll think twice about taking that first puff and readdicting yourself.

Take a deep breath and fill yourself with the pride of accomplishment of breaking free from this filthy and destructive habit.

QUITTER'S SURVIVAL GUIDE

A little friendly support to help you survive quitting smoking one day at a time.

NUTRITIONAL SUGGESTIONS

- Eat fresh foods—lots of fruits, vegetables, and whole grains.
- Don't skip meals.
- Supplement your diet with the vitamins mentioned earlier for the first 30 days after quitting smoking.
- Drink six to eight glasses of water a day.
- Exercise.
- Take a jacuzzi, hot bath, or sauna to help sweat out the toxins.
- Use oral or tactile substitutes to fill in the void with which not smoking leaves you.

WHAT TO DO WHEN THE URGE TO SMOKE HITS

- Don't panic. Urges are no threat to your success when handled effectively.
- Take a deep breath to the top of your head, and exhale the urge down through your body down into the ground.
- Use the Habit Breakers "pseudo-Lamaze" technique. Find a focal point, project the urge onto it, take a deep breath in through your mouth, and blow that urge farther and farther into space as you exhale.

- Use your Sense Memory, to recreate the "turn off" feelings about smoking.
- Fantasy Smoke a soothing white cloud, concentrating on the fresh, clean feeling of air in your chest—use a straw, or toothpick for an oral substitute if you like.
- Call someone and talk about your urge.
- Remind yourself to take frequent deep breaths throughout the day.
- Take a whiff of the jar of smoked butts.
- Remember your reasons for quitting smoking.
- Don't flirt with the desire to smoke. Stop the train of thought and move on to another thought or another activity.
- Brush your teeth.
- Take a shower.
- Leave the house for a quick walk or jog.
- Get busy with some work.
- Go to a place where smoking isn't permitted, like the movies.

Remember, you already made the decision to quit. The only thing left to do is follow through, handling each urge to smoke one urge at a time.

MAKE A COMMITMENT TO QUIT SMOKING FOR ANOTHER 24 HOURS. ALWAYS, ONE DAY AT A TIME!

THE HABIT BREAKERS PROGRAM

If you desire the additional help of an instructor-led program, individually or in a group, call 1-213-276-9707. Corporate plans are available, to be held on corporate premises.

Each program comes with a money-back guarantee.

COLISEUM BOOKS
1771 BROADWAY (AT 57TH ST.)
(212) 757-8381

59686   3/29/86

3 KICK IT   1@ 3.95 $3.95

                                             $3.95
TOTAL TAX $.35
CASH PAYMENT $4.30
CHANGE $.02

COLISEUM BOOKS
1771 BROADWAY (AT 57TH ST.)
(212) 757-8381

QUIT SMOKING USING THIS BOOK OR YOUR MONEY BACK!

If you have read this book and followed its advice for 5 consecutive days and still can't quit smoking, we'll refund the full purchase price of this book. Here's what you *must* do to get your money back:

1) Send the whole book and proof of purchase (cash register receipt) back to HPBooks, Dept. QUIT, PO BOX 5367, Tucson, AZ 85703.

2) Enclose a self-addressed stamped envelope with the book.

We will refund your purchase price in full (U.S. funds) within 60 days of receipt of book. Limit one refund per family.